Acknowledgements

This book could not have been produced were it not for the decades of experience and knowledge of NFIB's Washington, D.C., staff. Special thanks to: John Motley, Mike Rousch, Wendy Lechner, Mary Reed, Nelson Litterst, Mark Isakowitz, Kent Knutsen, Kim McKernan, Mary Reed, Harriet James, James Wickett and Dana Balbieri. Thanks also to David Cullen, Denny Dennis, Joanne Erickson, Kate Vislay, Pat Lawry and Kenneth Furlough. And to the nearly 1,000 other employees of NFIB. Thanks also to Rex Hammock, Adele Rowan, Bobby Stark, Bill Hudgins, Julia Evers, Michael Nott, Roger Clayton, Melanie Brogli and Shari Davis.

A Comprehensive Examination of the Major Governmental and Legislative Issues Affecting Small Business, from the National Federation of Independent Business, the Nation's Leading Small Business Advocacy Organization.

SMALL BUSINESS
How government is threatening your busines

UNDER SIEGE

What you can do to fight back and win.

EDITED BY JACK FARIS,
President & Chief Executive Officer
National Federation of Independent Business
Washington, D.C.

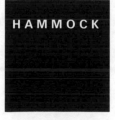

HAMMOCK

publishing inc.

NASHVILLE

National Federation of Independent Business
600 Maryland Ave. S.W.
Suite 700
Washington, D.C. 20024
(202) 554-9000

To order additional copies, call:
1-800-634-2669

For quantity sales information, contact:
Hammock Publishing Inc.
3322 West End Avenue, Suite 700
Nashville, TN 37203
(615) 385-9745

ISBN: 0-9635489-1-3

10 9 8 7 6 5 4 3 2 1

Manufactured in the United States of America

This book is dedicated to the
nation's small business owners,
America's most endangered species.

Contents

Introduction
1

Chapter 1
WHY WE SHOULD CARE ABOUT
SMALL BUSINESS
IN AMERICA
15

Chapter 2
HOW GOVERNMENT IS
BURYING SMALL BUSINESS
UNDER PAPERWORK
23

Chapter 3
HEALTH CARE:
SMALL BUSINESS SEARCHES
FOR A CURE
33

Chapter 4
TAXES:
GOVERNMENT'S IDEA OF
WORKING FOR A LIVING
75

Chapter 5
YOU PUT UP THE MONEY;
I'LL TELL YOU HOW TO RUN IT:
GOVERNMENT INTRUSION INTO THE WORKPLACE
93

Chapter 6
PROTECTING THE ENVIRONMENT,
BUT WHO WILL PROTECT SMALL BUSINESS?
109

Chapter 7
STATE GOVERNMENT:
PROOF THAT THE SIEGE CAN BE BROKEN
127

Chapter 8
HELP LIFT THE SIEGE ON SMALL BUSINESS –
WHAT YOU CAN DO
141

Chapter 9
SMALL BUSINESS SURVIVAL GUIDE
155

Chapter 10
OPINIONS OF SMALL BUSINESS OWNERS ON
KEY ISSUES FACING THE CLINTON
ADMINISTRATION AND THE 103RD CONGRESS
167

Chapter 11
CONGRESSIONAL DIRECTORY
185

Introduction

The mysterious package arrived in my mail a few weeks after I placed a small notice in an NFIB newsletter requesting examples how even the most well-intentioned government policy can pack a wallop for small business. Weighing about two pounds, nothing on the outside indicated its origin or sender. No name. No return address. With curiosity, I opened the box.

Inside, again with no letter or identification, I found hundreds of pages of government documents. I sifted my way through the stack and found a barrage of local, state and federal forms received by the business owner who sent me the package: instruction forms, applications, questionnaires, schedules, information forms, logs, data sheets, notices, reference guides, disclosure statements, reports, requirement guides, policy guides, restrictions, handbooks, pamphlets and requests.

With no explanation, the sender of this package clearly – and in this case, literally – spoke reams concerning the government's impact on small business. I could picture this frustrated business owner, spending each waking hour struggling to keep his or her American dream alive, brought up to believe that America rewards the risk-taking job creator. Yet here they are discovering that, rather than a pat on the back from their government, they are flooded with a raging river of regulatory paperwork piling on new policies to which they must adapt or risk penalty.

I'll admit the package put a knot in my stomach as I reflected on the years I spent as a small business owner coping with the same flow of government paper. However, in the case of my anonymous correspondent, he or she seems to have stopped responding to the government paperwork factory at some point, choosing rather to place the government mail in a drawer or box as a silent protest against a faceless bureaucracy.

(Let me quickly note, this is not a response I would recommend, as other letters I received demonstrated that small business owners should think twice before messing with faceless bureaucrats who have the authority of federal and state governments to impose penalties, fines and even prison terms.)

The box of forms he or she sent me spoke as clearly as any example I received that, contrary to the political rhetoric in support of the concept and dream of American entrepreneurship and free enterprise, state and federal governments are enacting and enforcing legislation which places higher and higher barriers on the highway to the American dream of business ownership. As represented in the box of government paperwork the business owner mailed me, politicians and bureaucrats have targeted small business owners as the means to solve problem after problem facing our society.

Got a problem? The Government Can Fix It.

Paperwork is but one weapon in the war big government seems to be waging on small business. Perhaps it is an unintentional war. I hope so, for I would not like to believe that the issues and examples we explore in this book are the results of a conspiracy to destroy the American dream of entrepreneurship. Yet they are the clearly destructive results of an apparently growing belief (more accurately, misbelief) in the government's ability to solve any problem in society. The belief – and its fallout – goes something like this: Isolate a problem, attract enough media coverage to get the problem labeled a "crisis"; develop a government program to solve the "crisis"; enact legislation to solve the "crisis"; create a long list of regulations to enforce the legislation; build up the bureaucratic infrastructure (including paperwork) necessary to enforce the regulations; reward bureaucrats for catching people not following the regulations.

And are the problems really solved? Rarely. And almost never with the impact promised by backers of the new government program. But rather than do away with the program as a failure, the backers ask for it to be expanded and for more stringent regulations.

Yet in this government war on society's problems, one result is sure: small businesses are getting killed. For it seems the "solution" to any problem involves just one more regulation on small business; one more government mandate; one more tax or tax increase.

Again, I am not necessarily suggesting there is a conscious conspiracy to destroy small businesses. Rather, I believe that well-intentioned individuals and groups, with their misguided belief in a government fix, have woven together a network of regulations, programs, and taxes – along with the bureaucracy and paperwork to enforce them – that is suffocating small businesses. And while I do not believe these backers of big government have necessarily declared a war on small business – they know that to do so would be as popular as declaring a war on apple pie – their actions nonetheless convey such an intent. And their success is resulting in an outright siege on small companies.

In America, the growing belief in a government fix for every problem is leading quickly to a system in which individuals who have never started or run a business are issuing regulation after regulation telling small business owners whom they can hire and what they must be paid. These same elected officials and bureaucrats – most of whom have never met a payroll – are piling on mandatory employee benefits, employment guidelines, workplace regulations and compliance paperwork overload.

This belief in a government fix for every problem has created a web of regulations and accompanying regulatory bureaucracy which often frightens the owners of even the fairest, safest and healthiest workplaces. It has created a system that can destroy jobs and family businesses in order to save drainage ditches and obscure fish.

This belief in a government fix for every problem has led us to a society in which the majority of American people, when asked, say without considering the broader implications that, yes, the government should require employers to provide this or that new benefit. (The misinformed assumption, of course, is that employers can provide these benefits with no impact on jobs or the salaries of current employees.)

In the end, this belief in a government fix for every problem is leading our nation to the ultimate choice between government dictates and the free market.

And the fate of small business is caught in balance. For small business, perhaps more so than any other segment of the economy, is totally dependent upon an environment of market-driven free enterprise. On the other hand, large corporations seem more easily to adapt, sometimes even thrive, when the government steps in to dictate the prices, conditions and structure of a marketplace.

This reality helped add to the uneasy feeling I experienced while watching the 1994 State of the Union Address when the camera focused on the First Lady and the seats of honor to either side of her. Sitting on her right was the CEO of General Motors representing Big Business. Sitting on her left was the President of the AFL-CIO representing Big Labor. And standing before the First Lady was the

President, delivering a one-hour address in praise of Big Government.

Big Business. Big Labor. Big Government. When they team up, it always results in big problems for small business. Whenever you see this trio singing in harmony, you can bet their song is one of new government security programs and the taxes to fund them. But the free enterprise system is not based on government-provided security, but rather on the freedom to follow a dream. The freedom to win or lose. The freedom to succeed or fail. The free enterprise system is based on an individual's responsibility – and opportunity – to be able to secure his or her own future.

These are the freedoms which propel most small business owners.

Perhaps it is with great irony that free enterprise and a belief in the market economy is winning out across the entire world while in America, the land in which the free market has flourished, many leading policy makers seem enamored with "other industrialized nations" and all the government-run or -mandated programs they offer.

A front page article in the March 4, 1994, *Wall Street Journal* sums up this ironic phenomenon, "In Europe, businesses trumpet the benefits of the American flexibility ... *Flexibilisierung*, or making the labor market more flexible, is the latest buzzword in Germany. In the U.S., however, it is the liberals in the Clinton administration and academia who look longingly at Europe ... ."

Sure, all those guarantees against failure and truckloads

of mandated employer-provided benefits sound great. But then, who is going to pay? The European model teaches us that anyone who needs a job will pay. For Europe has created no net new jobs during the past 15 years.

That's right. No net new job creation in the past 15 years and a growing rate of long-term unemployment. Indeed, European job growth has been so dismal that economists have coined a term for it: Eurosclerosis.

Yet this is the model many policy makers in Washington seem so desperate for us to follow. A model based on a laundry list of government-mandated employee benefits. Rampant regulation. Pervasive government intrusion in all facets of a company's operation to ensure the "welfare of the employee." But just remember, no net new job creation in 15 years.

The argument goes that the United States should have new laws requiring universal employer-provided health care or more generous family leave or a ban on replacing striking workers, "because other industrialized nations have them." Other industrialized nations? If they're talking about Europe, maybe this "other-industrialized-nations-crowd" hasn't heard: No net new job creation in 15 years.

Recent studies, even one produced by the European Community itself, conclude that joblessness in Europe is the result of the burdensome regulations and mandates imposed on employers. The governments of Europe regulate all aspects of the employer-employee relationship, making it virtually impossible in many instances to hire non-permanent employees or lay off unproductive ones. Generous mandated benefits add heavily to the cost of employment. At the same time, excessive long-term unemployment benefits provide no incentives for returning to work.

The European model, in other words, is a model which discourages the creation or growth of small businesses. The direct and indirect costs heaped on the act of employing people make the creation and growth of such businesses nearly impossible. Yet this is the model we are told we should follow.

Owners of a small business belong to a unique category in the U.S. economy: They create jobs. Good jobs. During the past decade, large U.S. corporations with their burdensome union-negotiated, European-style employment benefits have laid off millions of employees. Yet small businesses helped take up the slack and created most of the 18 million net new jobs in the United States during the 1980s. That's right, 18 million net new jobs during the 1980s, a decade marked by deregulation, rather than the currently in-vogue, European-model inspired employer mandate build-up.

Small businesses have been the salvation of the American economy during the past decade. They have created jobs in good times, and bad. Yet, this record still does not protect them from those who view the world through government regulation-tinted glasses. Indeed, the fact that small business is the only real job creating engine in the U.S. economy these days does not fit in well with the strategy of government build-up backers.

So what do they do? They try to re-write history. Or in some cases, just resort to fiction. For instance, AFL-CIO economist John Salusky was quoted in the *Wall Street Journal* in January 1994, as claiming the American public has been "hoodwinked" into thinking that smaller companies are the most beneficial force in the economy. His reasons? The smallest companies are not covered by federal safety laws, anti-discrimination policies or other government safeguards. In other words, they are not regulated or unionized enough. Arguing that shifting costs of health care to the shoulders of small business owners is a good idea, Salusky claimed such a new cost to small business will generate job growth at bigger companies with better pay and worker protections. "Big companies need fair and equal treatment," he argued.

Such lack of logic would seem comical if it were not so tragic. To say that jobs at small firms are "not beneficial" because they are not unionized is bad enough. However, to suggest that burdening the economy's primary job creation engine, small business, is good because it will somehow create jobs at bigger firms really reveals the agenda of big labor – and big business for that matter.

But I'll say this about Mr. Salusky, at least he had the honesty to clearly state what he believes, rather than the empty words and double-speak of so many elected officials. At least Mr. Salusky has the honesty to say he believes small businesses are not as good for the economy as big unionized businesses with government-mandated benefits. And while I strongly disagree with all he says, I appreciate his helping me to most clearly give you an example of what the real ideology is of those who lead the siege on small business. Big labor. Big business. Big government. When they team up to solve society's big crises, it only means big trouble for small business.

The goals of small business owners are simple. Rather than become global corporations, they simply want the freedom to grow their businesses. They want to keep their families fed and perhaps pass the enterprises along to the next generation. If running their own business were akin to playing baseball, they would not be thinking "gotta get a home run" every time they came up to bat. A walk or a single would be fine – and might fit their overall strategy better. But in America, small business owners know their next turn at bat could yield a home run, maybe with the bases loaded, even if it's the bottom of the ninth, two out and they're behind in the count. What they don't want is a government that changes the rules in the middle of their turn at the plate. A government that won't give them the chance to swing away – or that takes away the bat and clobbers them over the head with it.

By their nature, American small business owners are optimists. They would not risk their savings, in many instances their homes, their names and their futures, on starting and running a business unless they have faith in a system that allows them to seek the opportunity they believe to be within their grasp.

Place that faith under siege and you destroy the passion

that propels these risk takers. Try to solve all society's problems by loading them on their backs and the only result will be broken backs.

The Best Response: Fight back

Fifty-one years ago, a few small business owners saw the need to share the concerns of entrepreneurs with lawmakers in Washington and in the state capitals. They formed the National Federation of Independent Business. Today, that organization has more than 600,000 members, who are fighting back against those whose actions threaten America's free enterprise system. Our tenacity has not always made us the most popular group on Capitol Hill and in state capitols – "like pit bulls," a congressman was recently quoted in what I consider to be a compliment, surely unintentional.

Lawmakers know where the members of NFIB stand. Every two months, we send out a survey to all 600,000 members, questioning them on the pressing small business issues of the day. Each legislator receives a detailed summary of the survey results from small business owners in his or her district. (Recent results to these "Mandate Ballots" can be found at the end of this book.)

NFIB members work in every industry and trade. Male and female, they are of every ethnic background and religious belief. They belong to every imaginable political party, or refuse to belong to any. On issues not directly tied to their ability to succeed in a free enterprise system, their opinions scatter to the four winds. Yet when it comes to issues related to government intrusion on their ability to compete and win, NFIB members – as revealed in three decades of surveys – speak with a fairly consistent voice. In the 1993 book, *Small Business in the Clinton Years*, I listed the following bedrock concerns and beliefs shared almost universally by those who own and run the nation's small businesses. These truths still stand today:

•Small business owners believe the government that governs least, governs best. They resent the way elected officials – the same men and women who have allowed the government to spend absurdly beyond its means – are constantly enacting laws that result in reams of regulations and mandates dictating how a small business must be run.

•For this reason, small business owners almost universally agree that government – federal, state and local – should tax less and spend less. They are strong believers that the men and women who are elected to govern need to have the discipline to run a government that lives within its means.

•The supremacy of private property rights is nearly universally supported by small business owners. Small business owners are extremely patriotic, loyal citizens who are the first to support the common good, but they have worked hard to create and build what they have and are committed to passing it on to their children. Therefore, they greatly oppose measures by any level of government – even well-meaning measures – which result in the confiscation or devaluation of an individual's private property without equitable compensation.

•Perhaps the strongest thread of belief running through the hearts and souls of small business owners is a belief in the individual. They are kindred minds with small business owners like John Hancock, Benjamin Franklin and the farmers who in July 1776 risked their lives, their fortunes and their sacred honors by signing the Declaration of Independence. Today, the vast majority of small businesses are created not by individuals expecting it to grow into a global conglomerate, but by committed individuals dedicated to the American tradition of individual freedom and the right to determine one's own destiny.

This book raises concerns. But it is not just a book of fear. For as I have said, the fuel that propels small business owners is optimism. Sure, there is a war going on in which small business owners find themselves under siege. But by fighting together, small business owners are learning they can win. And in this war for small business and America's free enterprise system, there is no doubt who the heroes are. And it is to them, the risk-taking owners of America's small business, the custodians of the American dream, that this book is dedicated.

Jack Faris
April 15, 1994

1

Why We Should Care About Small Business in America

T here's something about presidential elections that makes optimists of us all. Maybe it's the new ideas, the confident promises, the cheers of the crowds. Maybe we're just blinded by all that confetti. But we still feel good. We vote and send government our "wake-up call." And we believe that, somehow, this time, this new crop of legislators and administration officials will listen.

But soon the optimism begins to fade. At this point, each American citizen must ask: Am I going to let those promises slip away and just chalk them up to so much campaign rhetoric? Or am I going to remind the folks in Washington, D.C., that I'm still waiting for them to fulfill their promises?

They need to be reminded. Seldom has a new administration moved so quickly to tighten the grip of government on small businesses. Proposing employer mandates to pay most of their employees' health care insurance premiums. Proposals for worker safety committees which could easily set the stage for union organizing. Calls for stricter environmental and workplace regulations. Higher taxes and endlessly growing paperwork. From the ramparts small business owners see, not the rockets' red glare of greater freedom, but the dull clouds of encircling bureaucracy.

The promises of the 1992 elections revolved around improving the economy – specifically, generating more jobs. Small business owners around the country warmed to that idea right away. Why? Because as part of the nation's undisputed job-creating engine, they hoped for the opportunity – through decreased government regulations – to grow their businesses and generate the jobs this country so desperately needs.

Sadly, their hopes are too often dashed because people, particularly people in government, tend to forget that the health of small business is a critical key to the nation's job growth. That forgetfulness (or denial) creates an obstacle on the road to prosperity for all Americans.

Perhaps a refresher course is required. Ninety-nine percent of all businesses in America are small businesses. That equals more than 5 million businesses, employing 59 million people, plus an additional 11 million self-employed Americans. Of those 5 million businesses, 60 percent have four or fewer employees. Ninety percent employ fewer than 20 persons, and 94 percent have less than 50 employees. These figures illustrate that, by sheer volume, small business dominates America's economic strength.

Indeed, between 1982 and 1990, small business accounted for two-thirds (67 percent) of all net new jobs in America. In fact, businesses employing fewer than 20 people were responsible for generating 51 percent of that increased employment. Is this some huge secret? Hardly. These statistics were part of the November 1992 report of the Congressional Joint Economic Committee. Pretty clear first-day instructions that were already waiting for the new Congress and the new administration.

But it's been some time since that first day. And since then, the folks in Washington have again been lulled into forgetfulness – and tempted by a siren call. A pervasive voice that makes lawmakers and administration officials decide that someone else should solve the nation's social problems. The call sounds noble. The uninsured need health care. The environment needs protecting. Workplace safety is important. We all agree with those statements. Then the siren closes the trap: Make the small business owners pay.

Whoa! Where's the logic in that? If small businesses are doing the majority of the hiring, shouldn't we make it easier for people to start up and operate more small businesses? If you pass legislation that only adds to a small business owner's paperwork and financial burden, that's less time and money that can be used to grow the business. And what started out as a lofty goal becomes a well-intentioned law or regulation, which ends up as another crushing load of paperwork, hassles and wasteful costs for the small business owner. Once again, the regulatory ball-and-chain drags down the country's hiring opportunities.

This is a lesson that affects everyone in America – everyone – not just small business owners. Because be assured, someone you know will one day – maybe today – need a job. And it doesn't take a rocket scientist to see that, for now, the mathematical probability lies with small business, from a mom-and-pop operation on the corner to the high-tech entrepreneur and everyone in between. But that probability is getting smaller, as more small business owners are forced to freeze hiring or lay off workers to keep the business afloat.

It used to be that owning one's own business was the American dream. Be your own boss. Carve out your own niche. Build your business to the top. And return a little something to the community. When did the dream distort into this frightening nightmare? One factor is the misleading perception that small business runs just like big business, only smaller. Nothing could be further from the truth. Small business is a unique animal.

For example, half of small business owners get into business with less than $20,000, most of which comes from personal or family savings. While most small business owners do not make a lot of money, 10 percent earn less than $10,000, surviving on cash flow, not profitability.

On average, small business owners earn about $40,000 annually in salary and profit. But even that modest amount is misleading. During the first years, many owners earn less than their workers do, while putting in many more hours. In addition to their administrative work, many owners work shoulder-to-shoulder alongside their employees to get the job done. Few have the time to waste filling out the mountains of forms and paperwork associated with every new regulation that comes down the pike.

Over time, many small business owners become all too familiar with "the Thursday night knot" in their stomachs, lying awake wondering what miracle will occur that will allow them to meet the payroll by morning. Sometimes it means forgoing a paycheck for themselves. And usually, any and every dime of profit is plowed right back into the company just to keep it afloat.

These aren't vague generalizations. There are real people behind these arguments. People like Diane Orlowski, who with her husband own J.F.D. Tube and Coil Products in Hamden, Conn. Tired of feeling the government's boot on her back, Orlowski (a former union shop steward) made government listen to her when she testified before U.S. Secretary of Labor Robert Reich's Labor Law Reform Commission in December 1993.

"Ten years ago, my husband, Joe, our friend, Frank, and I started out in a two-car garage with a couple thousand dollars, a few second-hand machines and some used office equipment," Orlowski testified. "For the first few years, we took minimal salaries, living on what would normally be considered poverty level income – and that was for a 70- to 80-hour work week. Our workers earned substantially more than we did, putting in about half the time. But this is our business, and we did what was required to make it a success."

Listening to the folks in Washington, D.C., you'd think all small business owners are out to make a buck by trampling the rights of their employees. They must be forced by law to create a decent working environment. Small business owners like Diane Orlowski answer: Get real!

"Contrary to what certain special interests may claim," she said, "small business owners do give to their workers when they can. But government regulations and laws are making it just too expensive a proposition.

"As we became more profitable, we voluntarily began adding benefits: company-paid medical insurance for employees and their dependents; life insurance; a profit-sharing and 401(k) pension plan; paid holidays and vacation days; unpaid leaves of absence with continuation of medical benefits and flexible work schedules. When we are profitable, we also give out year-end bonuses.

"However, it is becoming more and more difficult to continue to provide these benefits. For instance, the 401(k) program has become an administrative nightmare because of IRS regulation. It costs me about $1,500 to administer, then there are a myriad of different 'tests' the plan has to pass. Last year, we 'failed' a test, which cost me over $11,500."

Unfortunately, her story is not unique. These problems are all too common among small businesses, which by definition should have less trouble than larger organizations. Orlowski explained, "We develop much closer relationships than one would find in large businesses and in large labor organizations. We joke and we argue and we tolerate each others' idiosyncrasies. We discuss problems and ideas on a much more personal and informal level than either big business or big labor.

"For example," she said, "just this past winter, J.F.D. was in a major work slump. We were discussing the possibility of a four-day work week. We didn't want to lay anyone off. So nearly half the staff, including production workers, assisted with marketing to increase sales. The workers also agreed to postpone January reviews until times got better. By mid-February, sales started increasing, and our workers averaged more than a 5 percent raise.

"We need to remain flexible to grow and prosper. We cannot, nor should we, mandate relationships. Anymore than any one of us would want our marriage partner chosen for us, government should not require and micromanage our work relationships."

Orlowski concluded her testimony by saying that government could do more to help the people of this country by educating employees and employers about safety and health issues, by providing technical and capital support, and by training safety inspectors to be less adversarial in their approach. Such programs would be much more effective in stimulating America's job creating engine than across-the-board, one-size-fits-all mandates telling employers how they must run their businesses.

With the kinds of sacrifices and hassles that small business owners must endure, there is little wonder that of the 800,000 to 900,000 small businesses that start each year, half will be out of business within five years. Why should you care about them? Because as each one fails, more and more spouses, children and friends are out of work.

But most important, you should care because that's what Americans do. They care about injustice. They care about the little guy, struggling to succeed. They care about the American dream. Do they care enough to contact their state and federal legislators to tell them to ease up on the small business employers stuck between the bottom line and the unemployment line? They should. We'll see.

In his first inaugural address, President Thomas Jefferson (also a small business owner) advised Americans to seek, "… a wise and frugal government, which shall restrain men from injuring one another, which shall leave them otherwise free to regulate their own pursuits of industry and improvement, and shall not take from the mouth of labor the bread it has earned. This is the sum of good government, and this is necessary to close the circle of our felicities."

Today, government has forgotten Jefferson's advice. The siege of America's small business is slowly choking its ability to pursue "industry and improvement." Ask the former business owners and their former employees what government interference has done for them – their bread now comes from the unemployment lines.

The strength of America's economy lies in small business. This book is a call to action for citizens of this country to tell their lawmakers to stop burdening small businesses with new mandates and red tape. Rather, you should encourage – no, demand – that they help create an environment that will promote more jobs, from which we will all benefit.

2

How Government is Burying Small Business Under Paperwork

In the beginning God created heaven and earth. He was then faced with a class action suit for having failed to file an environmental impact statement with the Heavenly Environmental Protection Agency. God was granted a temporary permit for the heavenly portion of the project but was issued a cease-and-desist order to the earthly part, pending further study by HEPA.

After the smiles, small business owners may have cringed a bit when they read this excerpt from a 1992 Erma Bombeck column, reprinted from an anonymous essay appearing in the *Congressional Record*. The column goes on to recount God's hassles with obtaining water permits and game and fish commission permits, and with long waits for application reviews. After being told that a public hearing would have to be held, followed by 10 or 12 months before a permit could be granted, God finally changes his mind about creating heaven and earth and says: "To Hell with it."

For small business owners, the humor comes a little too close to home.

The Small Business Administration places the cost of regulation and paperwork on small business at about $100 billion a year, a figure that amounts to a huge tax on productivity. In addition, between 1987 and 1992, the federal paperwork burden, measured in hours, increased 261 percent, according to the General Accounting Office. Small businesses do not have the human or financial resources to absorb the paperwork burden. It is estimated they are hit three times as hard as other, larger businesses.

Recently, the NFIB Foundation commissioned a survey that asked small business owners to rank their biggest challenge. After taxes, they said regulations. A similar study by Arthur Andersen Enterprise Group ranked regulations number one. According to the study, business owners are likely to spend 10 percent of work time on regulations. Nancy Pechloff of Arthur Andersen summed up the opinion of most small business owners this way: "Regulations create a tremendous diversion of precious resources and involve time and personnel that could be devoted to bringing in new business (and providing government with more tax revenue)."

Government forms pile up in a small business owner's in-box like the mountains of direct mail merchandise catalogs most Americans receive at home. But don't look in these for inviting pictures of hiking boots or fresh fruit. Open them up and you are ordered to report obscure data for which you have no record.

24

Most small business owners view the government paperwork burden like the owner of an 18-employee chemical manufacturing company in Georgia who in April 1993, wrote the U.S. Bureau of the Census asking to be relieved of the responsibility of completing the Commodity Flow Survey she had just received. If this were the only form she had to contend with, "I might be able to handle completing it," she wrote.

"Our bookkeeping and tracking systems are not geared to handle this type of report without burdensome and manual handling of hundreds of pieces of paperwork," she said. Moreover, so that one agency could understand the cumulative impact of government paperwork on her firm, the small manufacturer sent to the Census Bureau a list of paperwork required of her by other agencies. Listed were hundreds of hours worth of Environmental Protection Agency reporting. There were reporting requirements from the Bureau of Labor Statistics, the Department of the Treasury and various paperwork requirements from the state of Georgia.

The business owner went on to list tax forms, INS immigration forms and the like. She also referred in her letter to Material Safety Data Sheets (MSDs), required by the Occupational Safety and Health Administration (OSHA). MSDs are technical documents that must be furnished by the business owner with every product used which may present some chemical hazard. In the case of the Georgia chemical manufacturer, she must send some 1,800 MSDs to each of her 650 customers, in addition to keeping a full set of these sheets on each company truck.

Most small business owners do not believe all government information collection is inherently bad. But they are deeply concerned that much of it is duplicative and impractical, and a harmful drain on a small firm's ability to produce, compete, pay its employees, pay taxes and make a living.

If there remains any doubt that small businesses in America are under siege – even if that siege comes as the result of actions taken by those who are unaware of the impact of their pet causes – a glance at the following list will give you some indication of the paperwork burden on the individuals who create the majority of America's new jobs. It is but a partial list of the forms they can expect to receive and explains why many small business owners feel buried by government paperwork.

Federal Business Forms and Information

IRS

Form 940: FUTA Tax Return
Instructions for Form 940
Form W-5: Earned Income Credit – Advanced Payment
    Certificate
Form W-4
Instructions on Business Expenses for Preparing
    Returns

Instructions on Depreciation for Preparing Returns

Form 8087: Request for Missing/Incomplete W-2/W-3 Information

Form 4598: Form W-2, W-2P, or 1099 Not received or Incorrect

Form 6450: Questionnaire to Determine Exemption from Withholding

Form 4669: Employee Wage Statement

Form 4419: Application for Filing Information – Returns Magnetically/Electronically

Form 4417-A: Request for Federal Tax Deposit Coupon Books

Form 2106: Employee Business Expenses

Form SS-8: Determination of Employee Work Status Purposes for Federal Employment Taxes and Income Tax Withholding

Instructions for Form 1065

Instructions for Forms 1120 and 1120-A

Instructions for Form 1040X

Instructions for Schedule 3 (Form 1040A)

Form 1099-MISC: Misc. Income

Form 1099-S: Proceeds from Real Estate Transactions

Form 5498: Individual Retirement Arrangement Information

Form 8608: Nondeductible IRA Contributions, IRA Basis, and Nontaxable IRA Distributions

Form 8582: Passive Activity Loss Limitations

Form 4684: Casualties and Thefts

Form 4562: Depreciation and Amortization

Form 1040: Schedule SE - Self Employment Tax
Form 1040: Schedule E – Supplemental Income and
    Loss
Form 1040A or 1040: Schedule EIC – Earned Income
    Credit
Form 1040: Schedule D-1: Continuation Sheet for
    Schedule D
Form 1040: Schedule D: Capital Gains and Losses
Form 1040: Schedule C: Profit or Loss From Business
Form 1040: Schedule A&B: Itemized Deductions and
    Interest & Dividend Income
Instructions for Form 1040A
Instructions for Form 1040
Form 8109: Federal Tax Deposit Coupon Instructions
    for Form 8582: Passive Activity Less Limitations
Instructions for Form 3468: Investment Credit
Instructions for Form 4797: Sales of Business Property
Form SS-4: Application for Employer ID Number
Instructions for W-2
Information on Self-Employment Tax
Form 1096: Annual Summary and Transmittal of US
    Information Returns
Instructions for Forms 1099, 1098, 5494, and W-2G
Form 8300: Reporting of Cash Payments over $10,000
    Received in a Trade or Business
Information on IRA's for Preparing Returns
Information on Business Reporting – Employment Taxes
    and Information Returns

Department of Labor

Regulations, Part 3: Payment and Reporting of Wages
    Applicable to Federally Financed and Assisted
    Construction Contracts

Regulations, Part 5: Labor Standards Provisions
    Applicable to Contracts Covering Federally
    Financed and Assisted Construction

Pamphlet: Your Rights as an Employee on a Federal or
    Federally Financed Construction Job

Employee Notice re. Federal Minimum Wage

Recordkeeping Guidelines for Occupational Injuries and
    Illnesses (OSHA)

Form: Supplementary Record of Occupational Injuries
    and Illnesses (OSHA)

Form: Log and Summary of Occupational Injuries and
    Illnesses (OSHA)

Form: Material Safety Data Sheet (OSHA)

Child Labor Regulations in Nonagricultural Occupations
    Under FLSA

Federal Child Labor Laws in Nonfarm Jobs

Final Rule: Occupations Particularly Hazardous for
    Employers of Minors 16-18

Final Rule: Applications of Employee Polygraph
    Protection Act

Employee Notice re Employee Polygraph Protection Act

Handy Reference Guide to FLSA

FLSA of 1938 (Revised 1991)

Tier One Instructions – Superfund Amendments (OSHA)

Tier Two Instructions – Superfund Amendments (OSHA)
OMB Disclosure Statement – Instructions for OSHA
Number 200

Environmental Protection Agency

Form: Application for Permit to Discharge – National
Pollution Discharge Elimination System.
Form: Application – Facilities Which Do Not Discharge
Process Wastewater
Form: Application – Wastewater Discharge Information
Form: Application for Discharge – New Sources and
New Discharges
Form: Application for Permit to Discharge Stormwater –
Discharges Associated with Industrial Activity
Policy Guide: Annual Toxic Chemical Release Inventory
Reporting
Commonly Reported Section 313 Chemicals
Section 313 Document Request Form
Form: Toxic Chemical Release Inventory Reporting
Final Rule: Full Text of EPA Emergency Planning and
Release Notification Requirements
Policy Guide: Magnetic Media Submission Instructions
Toxic Chemical Release Inventory – Section 313
Policy Guide: Reporting Emergencies: Section 304
Notification
Chemical Release Reporting Requirements and Toxic
Release Inventory Reporting

Standards Applicable to Generators of Hazardous Waste
Part 260 – Hazardous Waste Management System –
General
Part 268 – Land Disposal Restrictions

Equal Employment Opportunity Commission

ADA Handbook: Title I, Title III, and Appendix B
Part 1625 – Age Discrimination in Employment Act -
Interpretations
Part 1627 – Records to be Made or Kept Relating to
Age/Notices/Administrative Exemptions
Pamphlet: Age Discrimination
Form: Employer Information Report EEO-1
Employer Information Report Instruction Booklet
Laws Enforced by the EEOC
Guide for Preparation of an Affirmative Action Program
Pamphlet: Title VII – Enforces Job Rights

Department of Justice

Form: INS Employment Eligibility Verification
INS Handbook for Employers

Public Laws

Older Workers Benefit Protection Act
Abandoned Infants Assistance Act – 1991 Amendments
Employee Polygraph Protection Act of 1988

Social Security Administration

Form: Request for Information
Instructions for Form SSA – 7011 – F4
Form: Request For Earnings and Benefit Estimate
      Statement

3

Health Care:
Small Business Searches
for a Cure

Perhaps no other issue today presents more of a threat to U.S. small business than health care – or perhaps more accurately, health care reform. As we will show in this chapter, in many ways, small business owners are the *victims* of the nation's current health care payment system. Yet in its attempts to *solve* the current problems, the White House and others have devised plans that, if passed, will force many small businesses to stop hiring, let employees go, cut wages, forget growth plans or, possibly, close for good. Once again, the belief in a government fix for every societal problem could end up erecting even greater barriers in the already difficult road to the creation and ownership of a small business.

The issue of health care policy touches everyone, at the most personal possible level and often at the most trying of times. As will be seen, changing the manner in which health care is paid for and provided could literally remake our society.

Small business is at the center of the controversy

swirling around health care reform. For, as will be explained, due primarily to to a historic quirk in the nation's tax code, most Americans receive all or most of their health care coverage as a job benefit. Yet small business owners often find insurance coverage unaffordable, or even unobtainable. A major illness in the family of one employee can threaten coverage for the entire company. And a "preexisting" health condition can lock an employee into a job.

A trillion-dollar industry, health care comprises more than 14 percent of the U.S. economy. Industry analysts estimate that it will rise above 16 percent by 2000, as the population ages and demands more medical miracles to stave off illness and debility. Also driving the increase are the epidemics of AIDS, random violence and poverty-related diseases.

Who pays for all these health services? Ultimately, everyone does. Medicaid, Medicare and other tax-supported programs pay more than 42 percent, private insurance pays 33 percent and patient out-of-pocket payments account for around 20 percent of total health care expenditures, according to *Health Care Financing Review*. The cost of paying for the rest either is shifted to some other payer through higher fees or written off as charity care – and shifted to others in the same way.

And everyone, from the largest corporation on down, complains about the cost. Increasingly, big companies that can self-insure are revamping health plans to require employees to pay more out of their pockets. They also are moving into managed care plans that, while limiting the choice of physicians, appears to help control costs. Medium-size companies are contracting with managed care organizations seeking the same results. But the owners and employees of the smallest companies – the ones that create the most jobs – generally lack comprehensive coverage, if any at all. Not because small business owners don't want to offer it, but because they cannot get it or because it is cost-prohibitive.

Countless small business owners tell the same stories – they had insurance but their carrier canceled, refused to renew or drastically increased rates when an employee or dependent developed a serious illness. Other insurers refused coverage or offered it only at exorbitant rates. Or simply wouldn't talk to them at all. Says Mrs. Clarence McIlwain of Chimney Rock Air Conditioning in Bellaire, Texas: "We have joined the ranks of Americans without health insurance. When our premiums as owners of a small business are raised to more than 50 percent of our share of the profits of our company, which constitutes our total income, we had to cancel our health insurance."

With 38 million people lacking any health care insurance coverage, and millions more underinsured against serious illness, health care became a central issue of the 1992 presidential campaign. Then-candidate Bill Clinton vowed to produce a plan to guarantee coverage to everyone – primarily by requiring all employers not only to offer coverage but also to pay most of the price tag.

True to his promise, President Clinton in late 1993

unveiled a proposal for employer-sponsored health care that *Fortune* magazine has described as "slightly richer" than the average Fortune 500 company's plan, and "diamond-studded" compared to most companies' health plans. Carrying a price tag not even the administration was sure could be paid, and undergirded by a new, multi-layered bureaucracy, the Health Security Act promised universal coverage that would be affordable, high-quality and simple to obtain and administer.

If made law, the plan would immediately affect 99.9 percent of all U.S. companies and 71 percent of all American workers. The rest, comprising the country's largest employers – those with more than 5,000 employees – would be subject to increased regulation and taxation to help support the plan.

For small business, the Health Security Act represents a nightmare, since many of the uninsured and underinsured work for companies with fewer than 100 employees. The plan includes a mandatory "premium" – actually a payroll tax. Businesses must pay for 80 percent of the costs of all full- and part-time employees' health care insurance. They can then apply for subsidies that would limit the payroll tax to 7.9 percent or less. The plan requires employers to undertake extensive recordkeeping and reporting to a welter of local, state and federal agencies. And it provides that, if the government's estimates are off, business' contributions will go up, by increasing the premium (read "tax"), levying other taxes, or both.

As this book was going to press, the Clinton plan

appeared in critical condition. NFIB, which has for years been advocating market-based health care reform, immediately opposed the Clinton plan due to its dependence on employer mandates. In fact, NFIB has a 51-year history of opposing the ever-expanding intrusion of government control and regulation into all areas of the economy. With the passage of the Clinton plan, the federal government would control and regulate another one-seventh of the U.S. economy. After a year of NFIB's unwavering opposition to the employer mandates contained in the Clinton plan, several other major business groups began to make their opposition known. Responding to pressure from its members, the U.S. Chamber of Commerce, which had earlier supported employer mandates, withdrew its support of the plan. The Business Roundtable and the National Association of Manufacturers also weighed in with their opposition.

However, during his first year in office, President Clinton showed a remarkable talent for salvaging seemingly moribund legislation through deal-making and compromise. Several competing proposals on Capitol Hill could give him some maneuvering room. And lawmakers are feeling pressure from constituents to resolve major issues such as health care.

Constituents like Lilly Teslow, who operates Teslow Co. in Loves Park, Ill. She says the 47-year-old company has offered health care for more than 40 years. "In the beginning, we were able to pay for all of it, employees and dependents. As the employees got older, we had to drop the dependent part and employees paid that through payroll deductions. Now, we are having to pay huge amounts and we can't change because of preexisting conditions on almost everyone. We need help to change to a better plan at less cost that will cover everyone. Loyal employees must be covered with health insurance even when they get older and develop problems."

Small businesses want health care coverage for themselves and their employees. They say it should be portable, renewable, guaranteed and affordable. What businesses small or large don't want is a larger, more intrusive government trying to manage something it has shown no ability to manage. There are steps that can be taken to reform the health care system in this country – without turning it into another massive, open-ended entitlement program financed by employers.

Managing the Health Care Reform Vocabulary

With the move toward health care reform, a new vocabulary appeared. It has left many Americans vainly thumbing their dictionaries trying to keep up with the latest Washington techno-jargon and acronym-speak. The following medical dictionary of health care debate terms may help you evaluate the cures.

Managed Competition
A key reform option intended to inject more competi-

tion into the health insurance market. Supporters say the establishment of managed competition will create local, competitive health care markets and educate and empower consumers to make more cost-conscious decisions about their own health care. In a managed competition system, small businesses and individuals would band together into large purchasing groups (see HIPCs) to increase their buying power. Providers of medical services (see AHPs) would compete for the group's health care business.

Health Alliances, or Health Insurance Purchasing Cooperatives (HIPCs)

HIPCs (pronounced HIP-icks) are groups of health care consumers (businesses and individuals) who purchase insurance as a bloc to obtain reasonably priced, quality health care. As in any free market, doctors, hospitals and other providers (see AHPs) compete for the HIPCs business by offering a better product (quality and range of services) at a better price. In addition, say those who devised the concept, by pooling the purchasers, HIPCs would reduce redundant administrative costs.

Accountable/Approved Health Plans (AHPs)

AHPs refer to health care provider groups, that is, hospitals, groups of doctors, insurance companies and managed care companies. In managed competition, AHPs compete to provide the highest-quality, lowest-cost health care to members of a HIPC. Under the Clinton plan, all

AHPs would offer a standard benefits package, defined by the government. Members of the purchasing pool receive a list of AHPs from which to choose, along with cost and quality data on each one.

Closed AHPs

Closed AHPs are essentially self-insured companies that serve as their own insurance provider and do not join a health insurance purchasing group. Large corporations, for example, have the broad employee base needed to assume their own insurance risks and serve as a closed AHP.

Managed Care

Managed care is a term used for the organization and coordination of health care providers into a single, cost-effective system. Central to managed care is the concept of a "gatekeeper," who serves as the monitor/coordinator of care and decides when specialists are needed above and beyond primary care. Different types of managed care include:

Health Maintenance Organizations (HMOs), the most common form of managed care. There are no deductibles and only modest copayments. This encourages patients to have more regular check-ups and screenings and to seek treatment early, before a mild condition worsens into a more costly one. The system also gives doctors a financial incentive to focus on preventive care (less work, same pay), which lowers overall health care costs. Foster Higgins, a nationally known benefits consulting firm, found that HMOs in 1993 cost an average of $3,276 per person – a 6.5 percent increase over the previous year, based on a survey of 2,395 employers. This was $224 less than traditional indemnity insurance plans, whose costs rose 7.1 percent.

Preferred Provider Organizations (PPOs), combine the features of HMOs and fee-for-service plans, allowing patients to see doctors outside their chosen health care plan for a higher fee. A popular type of **PPO** arrangement is the "point of service" option, which grants even more flexibility and choice to consumers by allowing them to use doctors outside the network, but provides strong financial incentives, through lower copayments, to use affiliated doctors. Costs per person for 1993 averaged $3,317, a 5.5 percent rise over 1992, according to the Foster Higgins survey.

Medical Savings Accounts

Also known as Medical IRAs or Medisave Accounts, medical savings accounts are a means to provide a personal, portable savings account for an individual's medical expenses. Individuals or employers can make tax-free deposits into these accounts, just as they would an individual retirement account (IRA). Supporters claim that by controlling their own medical payments, individuals would make more cost-conscious decisions and save on administrative costs.

Global Budgets

Global budgets are national spending limits for health care services. In most proposals calling for global budgets, both public and private health spending would be capped by a national board in order to bring health care spending down and force lower costs. The responsibility for issuing and enforcing price controls would be either at the state or the federal level. The obvious problem with a global budget, say its many detractors, is that it leads to rationing of health care.

Community Rating

Currently, insurance carriers set premiums based on an individual's or group's specific health risks and medical history. Community ratings would mean every business and individual in a geographic area would have the same premium, regardless of the health status of its employees.

Modified Community Rating

Rather than a pure community rating in which all individuals are given the same premium rate, modified community ratings allow insurance premiums to be adjusted for age or gender.

Tax Cap

Under the current system, incorporated employers are allowed to deduct everything they spend on health insurance premiums for their employees. Similarly, employees are not taxed on the value of the health insurance given to them by their employers. As a result, employers and individuals have less of a stake in what they pay for health care. A central idea in most of the currently proposed forms of managed competition would allow employers to deduct (for tax purposes) only the cost of the average basic health care plan in their area. Similarly, employees would be taxed on any coverage above and beyond the basic plan. The tax cap is an effort to make both employers and employees more cost-conscious about their health care decisions. Also, it is believed that the taxes on those benefits above the standard benefit plan would help fund coverage of those who are currently uninsured.

Single Payer System

Also called "nationalized health care," it is the system now used in Canada. Under this system, the federal government would pay for all health services. Individuals would simply go to the doctor or hospital of their choice and the government would pay the bill. To finance such a system, taxes would have to be significantly increased.

Health Care in America: a clinical overview

America's current health care industry is one of the most complex socioeconomic systems in the world. At its best, it provides medical care that would have seemed almost magical only a few decades ago. At its worst, it is vulnerable to high prices, fraud and abuse, and unequal access. It would take a separate book to trace all the roots of the modern health care industry, and that is not the purpose here. But it may be useful to take a quick overview so owners of small businesses can understand why they are being targeted as the "natural" source for health care coverage.

Origins of employer-sponsored health care coverage

The concept of employer-sponsored health care insurance coverage arose during World War II, when the federal government froze wages to control inflation. Unions pushed for new non-wage benefits in contracts, such as health care insurance coverage.

These benefits received a legal boost in the 1940s when the Internal Revenue Service ruled that large employers could deduct health care insurance benefits as a cost of doing business. At the same time, the IRS said employees did not have to report those benefits as taxable income.

As a result, health insurance benefits proved very popular among workers and soon became a standard element in collective bargaining for unions. Employers also felt health plans were a relatively inexpensive way to recruit and retain choice employees.

Most plans of the time covered primarily hospitalization for serious illnesses, instead of the wide, often state-mandated, menu of services most plans contain today. These group hospitalization plans came into being during the Depression, when hospitals began offering them as a source of revenue, as well as to help impoverished families afford basic, limited inpatient hospital care. Baylor University Hospital in Dallas is credited with offering the first such plan, which was widely copied and eventually led to the creation of Blue Cross.

During and after World War II, the price of such benefits seemed minimal. Health care was far less sophisticated and costly than today. Employers felt more confident about passing along the costs of generous benefit plans to consumers. Health benefits were sweetened over the years, through collective bargaining in unionized businesses and in response to competition for employees elsewhere.

As a result, fringe benefits such as health care coverage have become a major cost of doing business.

Today, according to industry estimates, nearly three-quarters of all employed Americans enjoy their health care coverage through employers. And since the value of these benefits is not considered income for employees, American workers received nearly $67 billion in federal tax breaks (in 1991) and several more billion in state tax breaks – and most never realized they had this "invisible" fringe benefit. Most employees also don't realize that such benefits are part of their total compensation, that is, that every dollar spent on insurance premiums is one less dollar in their hands. Despite the tax break, employees sometimes prefer to risk being uninsured in order to increase their take-home pay. Charles Anderson, a veterinarian in

Waco, Texas, says he used to offer health care benefits to his employees, but they voted to take the value of the premiums in salary instead.

Most employees also don't realize how valuable these benefits are in protecting them from the full cost of health care. In 1950, patient out-of-pocket payments covered two-thirds of the bills, but today patients pay only about 20 percent. Private insurance pays about 33 percent.

But employers know the value, and cost, of these benefits all too well. In today's economy, they also know they can no longer easily pass continually rising costs on to consumers and remain competitive. Large businesses have in recent years tried to hold down costs by more closely controlling employee access and use of health care. According to the Health Insurance Association of America, over half of the American workforce is employed by companies that are somewhat or totally self-insured.

Being self-insured exempts these companies from having to provide many of the state mandated services small businesses have to contend with through private insurance. There are some legal precedents that appear to allow self-insured companies great flexibility in changing benefits for individual employees, such as those who contract AIDS, in order to limit how much the health plan would have to pay.

Larger companies have also contracted with or helped create managed care companies, such as health maintenance organizations (HMOs) and preferred provider organizations (PPOs). These arrangements limit choice of physician to those who have agreements with the managed care organization, unless the patient is willing to pay extra to see a doctor outside the group. Patients are also required to pay part of the cost of care, in an effort to force them to consider whether they really need to see a doctor.

These private market efforts have paid off. KPMG Peat Marwick reported that business health care premiums went up 8 percent from 1992 to 1993, a big improvement over the 11.5 percent increase the preceding year.

Still, costs keep going up. And some big businesses blame at least some of the continuing rise on small businesses that don't offer health insurance coverage. Large businesses say doctors and hospitals shift the costs of care for the uninsured and underinsured to those who do pay. If every employer offered health care insurance, they argue, there would be fewer unreimbursed costs to shift.

Make small businesses pay – and pay, and pay ...

Small businesses provide the bread and butter for the health insurance market. However, small business owners say that when it comes to purchasing and keeping health insurance, they're toast.

Most small business owners have experienced sudden policy cancellations or drastic premium increases when someone becomes seriously ill. They tell about being refused coverage by other insurers or offered it at a price far beyond reach. And they tell about having to accept wide-ranging policies containing coverages dictated not by their needs, but by a basket of specific benefits loaded up by state mandates.

Employees have their own horror stories to tell – of "job-lock," being unable to change jobs for fear of losing some or all of their health insurance; of large increases in their share of premium payments; of diminished access to health care services.

In 1993, the Employee Benefit Research Institute estimated that businesses with fewer than 50 workers employ about 40.2 million people, of whom one-fourth – 10.5 million employees – lack health insurance coverage. About 75 percent of companies with under 100 workers do offer coverage, and almost 90 percent of those with more than 100 employees sponsor coverage, according to industry estimates.

Not surprisingly, the smallest firms are the least likely to offer insurance benefits. Some 3 million firms – representing 60 percent of the total number of American businesses – employ four or fewer people. Of those, 76 percent do not offer health care insurance, according to the Health Insurance Association of America.

Cost is the chief problem. In 1993, Foster Higgins, one of the nation's top benefits consulting firms, found that the cost of employer health care benefits averaged $3,781 – an 8 percent boost over 1992. That was actually encouraging news, since it indicated costs increases were slowing. Between 1987 and 1991, the cost of insuring a single employee rose 79 percent (72 percent for family coverage). As a percentage of revenues, these costs are much more of a burden for small businesses than for larger companies.

Notes Troy Elliott of Troy's Welding Inc. in Albuquerque, N.M., "Our existing insurance costs are now 9.87 percent of our gross sales … . There is no way this business can produce enough revenue to cover all insurance costs, pay all state, federal and local taxes, and remain in business. If required to close, it will add nine more people to the unemployed group, having a small direct effect on our local economy."

Besides being able to absorb the outright cost of insurance, large incorporated businesses also can fully deduct contributions to health care plans from profits, reaping significant tax breaks not available to small, unincorporated businesses.

So, although small businesses represent a huge potential market for insurers, like Rodney Dangerfield, they get no respect. Their size and the structure of the insurance market are the reasons. Individually, a small business provides an insurer with a relatively tiny amount of revenue but a huge potential risk if someone gets sick. Many insurers engage in what is called "cherry-picking" or "cream-skimming" – covering only companies with young, healthy workers but declining coverage for small firms with older workers, for their dependents, or for individuals in the group who represent a high risk factor.

These are not "Cadillac" plans. Many require substantial copayments by employees, such as the plan Dean Gillespie's Bridge Builders Inc. in McMinnville, Tenn., has.

"Bridge Builders Inc. is struggling to continue furnishing health care insurance for employees and families – with employees sharing one-half the cost. Today, if we were required to do much more than we're already doing, then we may as well close the doors and let the government take care of us," said Gillespie.

If small businesses could join together to purchase insurance as a group or to contract with managed care organizations, more would be able to afford coverage. This has happened in some areas. It requires tremendous cooperation among businesses, insurers and health care providers. It is not always possible, as some states prohibit managed care practices as being anti-competitive.

Repeatedly, surveys show most small business owners would like to offer health care coverage benefits – indeed, they'd like to have coverage themselves. Ideally, they want health insurance coverage that is flexible, portable if employees change jobs, guaranteed renewable and, above all, affordable. What they don't want is a health insurance reform that forces them to choose either to offer health insurance coverage at high cost or go out of business.

Said Ben Satterfield who operates Mug-a-Bug Pest Control in Lawrenceville, Ga., an 18-year-old company with 10 employees: "I was able to purchase health care for my employees recently (70/30). If I had been forced to purchase it last year, I would have had to lay off people or go out of business."

Unfortunately, too many so-called reforms would force just that choice on countless small business owners.

50

The Health Care Reform Debate

The debate over American health care started long before the 1992 presidential campaign. Reform efforts date back at least to the administration of President Harry Truman, who wanted to nationalize care. Some 20 years later, President Richard Nixon considered instituting a play-or-pay system – requiring employers either to offer coverage ("play") or pay a tax to support public care programs.

Play-or-pay is still part of the health care reform debate, as are employer mandates. It is instructive to note that President Nixon also attempted unsuccessfully to control the economy with wage and price freezes – a key tactic in the Administration's plan to contain health care spending.

President Lyndon Johnson's Medicaid and Medicare programs stand as the only major national health care initiatives since the Truman years. And, despite repeated efforts to control costs, the price tags on these Great Society era programs have ballooned.

In 1965, the federal government projected that in 1990, Medicare would cost $9 billion. The actual cost was $106 billion – an error of 1,110 percent.

For Medicaid, which in 1965 was estimated to cost $1 billion in 1990, the real cost was $76 billion – a 7,600 percent error. The history of these programs casts serious doubt on the promises of government today that it will be able to efficiently manage rising costs in a trillion-dollar industry.

Verdict: Small business does have a health care crisis

Pundits and politicians can argue endlessly over whether there is a national crisis, but most small business owners would agree that they have a health insurance crisis on their hands. And the causes of their difficulties mirror the reasons most frequently cited to justify reform:

•Costs. Health care costs have been doubling every seven years. American health care is among the best in the world – in quality, convenience, and availability and access to technology. This all comes at an increasing price, which drives up the cost of insurance. Many polls show that most Americans would not willingly trade quality and ready access to technology or the doctor of their choice for lower premiums.

•Lack of any or at least adequate coverage: Some 38 million people lack health care insurance coverage, either through employers or some publicly funded program; many of these are dependents of working people. An additional, undetermined number of people have limited coverage that leaves them unprotected in the event of serious illness. These groups include many small business owners, as well as employees.

•Access to health care: Lacking adequate health insurance, the uninsured or underinsured often use the most expensive alternative – hospital emergency rooms – for primary as well as more serious medical care needs. Hospitals "shift," or pass along, these usually unreimbursed costs in the form of higher rates to paying patients.

As a result, insurance premiums and out-of-pocket payments also rise.

•Portability: Changing jobs usually means changing health care benefits – sometimes even the loss of some or all of the coverages one previously had. No other form of insurance is tied so directly to the workplace. Some surveys indicate as many as 20 percent of employees would like to change jobs but are afraid to lest they lose health care benefits. This "job-lock" limits the ability of small businesses to attract and keep good employees – indeed, it inhibits entrepreneurial workers from starting their own businesses. And in today's downsizing economy, countless workers may be only a pink slip away from being totally uninsured.

•Renewability: Years ago, insurers based their group premium rates on the general health and make-up of communities, a practice called community rating. As our society and medicine changed, in order to limit risk and improve profits, insurers began to figure premiums based on smaller groups. They limited their risks by charging more to insure relatively less healthy groups or by selectively insuring only the lowest-risk groups and individuals. Today, a serious illness in a small group can cause drastic premium increases or cancellation of coverage.

Most health care reform proposals attempt to address these issues, although in quite different ways. As seen in the pages that follow, the cures set forth in some proposals would be far worse than the disease.

The White House's Health Security Act

Although on the ropes at press time, the Clinton Administration's Health Security Act shouldn't be counted out yet. Congress is feeling pressure to do something about health care and, with a White House ready to deal, some of the negative elements of this plan could survive.

The Health Security Act claims to use market forces and managed care principles to hold costs in check while extending health care coverage to all. Everyone would be required to buy health insurance. Most would join groups called health alliances that would contract with health care providers for services. Emphasis would be on primary and preventive care, with access to specialists tightly controlled. There is no guarantee of choice of doctor. Price and spending caps abound, as do controls on premiums and doctor and hospital fees, and possible rationing of services to meet budgets.

From a small business point-of-view, the Health Security Act could as well be called the Business Insecurity Act, for the following reasons:

•Employer mandates: The White House plan would require all small employers to pay for health insurance for all full-time and many part-time and seasonal employees, and to contribute to Medicare for employees over 65.

•The plan calls for a new payroll tax. Employers must pay for 80 percent of employees' health insurance, applying for subsidies that would limit the payroll tax to 7.9 percent or less. Like any other payroll tax, it must be paid regardless of the business' financial situation. It increases the cost of hiring or keeping employees and will reduce wage increases, and probably wages.

•A study commissioned by NFIB and conducted by Consad Research Corp. found that at least 850,000 mostly low-paying jobs would be lost if the Clinton plan is approved. It also estimated that the proposed small business subsidies would total about $81 billion in 1996 alone and could be far higher if the reform effort fails to achieve its projected savings. Yet, without the subsidies, the job loss from the employer mandate could amount to more than 3.8 million, according to the study. Administration officials, of course, disputed these figures. Treasury Secretary Lloyd Bentsen said the plan would have no impact on the ov erall employment rate, stating that there would be "some shifting of jobs," but no net job loss.

•The Congressional Budget Office, which was critical of White House efforts to avoid calling the premium a tax, predicted relatively little employment loss. The CBO provided a setback to the proposal when it refused to allow the White House to disguise new taxes as mandatory "premiums," and thus avoid placing the cost of the health care program on the budget. Further, the CBO predicted that, by whatever name, the funding needed had been underestimated by at least $15 billion annually.

•The plan gives the government almost total control of 14 percent of the U.S. economy.

•The plan creates a vast new, multi-layered, $2 billion a year (at least) bureaucracy.

•The bureaucracy would demand unending streams of paperwork, record-keeping and reporting of employee data and business information, to assure compliance.

•The plan proposes to bring more independent contractors under the health care coverage umbrella, and gives the IRS power to rule on independent contractor status.

•States could decide to leave the system and set up single-payer, Canadian-style plans.

•Employers could bear additional financial burdens if health plans run into trouble.

•Only the largest companies (5,000-plus employees) could self-insure, and there is no flexibility to customize benefits or premiums.

•For two-worker families, both employers would pay premiums.

•There is little provision for medical malpractice reform.

The Health Security Act would affect 99.9 percent of all U.S. companies and 71 percent of all American workers. The rest, comprising employers with more than 5,000 employees, would face increased regulation and taxation to help support the plan.

An NFIB analysis has shown that 60 percent of health care funding in the Clinton plan would come from taxes on business – the Administration calls these mandatory payments "premiums." This would add up to a net increase of at least $29 billion in health care coverage costs to business the first year, according to a recent study by Lewin/VHI, a health care policy consulting firm. Small businesses would bear most of the burden. Since many of these small businesses do not presently offer health insurance, the payments would constitute a new, major tax.

"According to the premium amounts published under Clinton's proposals (assuming we pay 80 percent of $4,200 family premiums for all 43 of our married employees)," said Jack Miner of Timber By-Products Inc., in Albany, Ore., "our medical premiums would increase $77,360 a year. This represents an 84 percent increase! If our premium requirement is capped at 7.9 percent of payroll, our annual premium would increase $44,300. This would be a 48 percent increase!"

Employees who are not used to paying for insurance coverage would be in for sticker shock if they had to begin paying up to 20 percent of their premiums. Analysts estimate the average married employee will pay $872 a year. The lowest-paid workers may be eligible for government assistance in paying their premiums.

Originally, the Clinton Administration estimated that the average premium for a single person would be $1,800; and for a family of four $4,200. But the Lewin/VHI study concluded individual premiums would be $2,732, while family coverage would cost $5,975. About 44 percent of all Americans would pay more for health insurance, the Lewin study predicted, with 14.6 percent paying an additional $1,000.

Proponents of the Administration plan note that it caps the premium/tax at 7.9 percent of payroll, with temporary subsidies available for the smallest businesses. But the

Congressional Budget Office predicts the government has underestimated by up to $72 billion the total subsidies needed over the next five years. Congress can also lift the caps if the plan begins to run out of money.

If forced to provide health care, many small business owners will try to reduce their workforce as much as possible to minimize the cost. Since the cost of benefits for lower-paid employees is relatively high compared with their wages, those workers will be among the first to be laid-off or given reduced hours. A September 1993 Gallup Poll commissioned by NFIB asked small business owners what would be the effect of a premium that increased payroll costs 3.5 percent (with subsidies, the best case scenario for small businesses). One-third said they would let employees go. Half said they would have to raise prices.

Small business owners continue to speak out about the impact of this program. "I am a small business owner (25 employees) working very hard alongside my husband to build a future for ourselves," said Diane M. Weidrick of Tipndi, Inc., who operates the Tallmadge Dairy Queen in Cuyahoga Falls, Ohio. "We do not have a profit margin to support the President's proposed 80 percent burden of health insurance costs. Even with the proposed subsidies, a 3.5 percent rise in payroll costs will seriously challenge our ability to stay in business.

"We've considered cutting our staff, freezing all wage increases indefinitely and raising our prices. Also we could not invest in new equipment, store upgrades.... There would be no money left for these things.

"I haven't even mentioned the desire to eventually begin receiving an income from all of our hard work."

The hardest hit would be retailers and others who rely heavily on part-time workers. Only about 20 percent of part-time employees have employer-sponsored health insurance; many retailers say they cannot afford to insure all part-timers, even on a pro-rata basis.

Profits also would suffer, depending on how well a business could trim cost increases or pass them along to customers. As has been shown in the past decade, higher health care costs would have a chilling effect on wage increases, as well as on the ability of a business to grow.

Although small businesses would initially bear the brunt of the Clinton plan, larger companies that self-insure oppose it for similar reasons. While not being forced to join a health alliance, these companies would be assessed a 1 percent payroll tax to subsidize indigent and low-wage worker care, research and other costs of the national health plan. They would also have to set up reserve funds for health care and contribute to a National Guaranty Fund that would bail out bankrupt health plans. And they would be subject to taxes to help insolvent alliances continue to operate.

The government also would more tightly regulate self-insured companies. For example, they would be required to offer at least three different health care plans equal to the basic national benefit package.

Some analysts believe that these large companies would drop their self-insured status and let employees join the local health alliances. For the biggest companies, this could be the most cost-effective approach.

For these reasons, big business in January 1994 sided with small businesses in rejecting the Clinton plan as unworkable and as ultimately harmful to business.

The Clinton Plan: Opposition Grows

Because of its dependence on employer mandates (among other reasons), opposition to the White House plan grew among groups familiar with its potential impact on small business and job creation. Besides the early and unwavering opposition by NFIB to the plan's employer mandate provision, momentum against the plan has shifted in other ways:

•The American Medical Association, which had formerly endorsed employer mandates, modified its position in response to member protests. NFIB had been invited to consult with physicians in local chapters prior to the AMA's annual policy-setting meeting in December 1993. Following these informational meetings, the group voted to retreat from its support of mandates.

•The board of directors of the U.S. Chamber of Commerce at first endorsed employer mandates, but then withdrew and later opposed them in response to member demands.

•The Jackson Hole group, a prominent health policy group that originated the "managed competition" idea in health care, met in early 1994 and decided to modify its long-held support of employer mandates.

•The National Governor's Association, which had consulted for more than a year with NFIB about the potential consequences of the proposal, came out in favor of a reform plan that did not include employer mandates.

•The Business Roundtable rejected the plan in favor of a much more modest one put forth by Rep. Jim Cooper, D-Tenn., and Sen. John Breaux, R-La.

•The National Association of Manufacturers also rejected the White House's plan and employer mandates.

•Despite intense courting by both the President and First Lady, the American Association of Retired Persons declined to endorse the plan.

But what about Hawaii?

Backers of employer mandated health care coverage often cite Hawaii as a place where the approach has worked. For almost 20 years, Hawaii has pursued the goal of affordable, universal health care coverage through employer-sponsored insurance. It still hasn't achieved this elusive goal, and appears unlikely to do so any time soon.

By law, there is nearly universal health coverage for

employees working 20 hours or more a week – although employers are not required to cover dependents. Health insurance premiums average far less than those on the mainland. Premiums are essentially community-rated, spreading the risks and costs. There is Medicaid for the poor, and a copayment/ deductible system for those not otherwise covered, affording basic coverage with highly restricted benefits.

The system stresses and encourages preventive care – and infant mortality rates and life expectancy are among the best in the nation.

At first glance, Hawaii would appear to prove that employer mandates work, even for small companies. Indeed, most of Hawaii's economy is composed of small businesses – there are more than 27,000 with fewer than 50 employees, according to the state department of labor.

But Hawaii is unique. Its location makes for a tight, competitive labor market that encourages employers to offer attractive benefits for recruiting and retaining good workers. With tourism one of the primary industries, it's relatively easy to pass along the cost of such benefits. Permanent residents just have to put up with Hawaii's cost of living, which is 30 percent higher than the average on the mainland.

Despite its advantages and a score of years of trying, Hawaii still has not managed to bring health care coverage to all its residents. And its health care costs are rising rapidly, faster even than on the mainland.

In the final analysis, then, Hawaii has not found a

health care paradise. And like a tropical flower, its approach cannot be readily transplanted back to the mainland.

Cooper/Breaux Managed Competition Plan

After big business joined small business in rejecting the Administration's plan in January, national attention turned to the "managed competition" proposal sponsored by Rep. Jim Cooper, D-Tenn., and Sen. John Breaux, D-La. Based on the health plan long enjoyed by federal employees, including members of Congress, there was much in this plan for small businesses to like.

The Cooper/Breaux bill contains no employer mandates. It restructures health insurance, allows for greater consumer choice and, its sponsors say, costs far less than the White House plan. Cooper says the proposal will cost $25 to $40 billion a year – not peanuts, but barely an *hors d'oeuvre* compared to the more than $140 billion it is estimated the Clinton plan would cost.

Under this plan, health cooperatives, similar to rural electric power co-ops, would be formed to coordinate, purchase and manage access to health care plans and services. The co-op informs residents in its coverage area of the various plans available, and their prices, comparative quality based on set of standards, and customer satisfaction ratings. The co-op also enforces standards and regulations, reviews treatments provided and the outcomes, and conducts quality and customer satisfaction surveys.

Each plan offers the same comprehensive list of services, but may use different doctors and hospitals and
charge different premiums – not unlike competing stores
offering the same merchandise but at different prices.
Residents choose plans annually. Since there is expected
to be overlap of doctors and hospitals in competing plans,
you could theoretically switch plans but continue to see
the same doctor. Or if your doctor drops out of one plan,
you could move to another to stay with that physician.

As in other managed care systems, health care
providers compete with each other to provide the best
quality for the lowest cost.

Insurance premiums would be community-rated, based
on the co-op's coverage region, not on small groups.
Insurance companies would have to offer policies to
everyone in that area, regardless of age, sex, health condition or employment, at a low group rate. Insurers could
not deny or drop coverage to people who changed jobs or
became ill.

Employers who offer coverage get tax incentives.
Deductions for large companies would be limited to the
value of the basic plan in that area. Workers whose
employers do not offer insurance could purchase a policy
and deduct the premium from their taxes. The indigent
and those below a certain income level would receive sub-
sidized care, while Medicaid would be abolished.
Preventive care would be encouraged by eliminating
copayments and deductibles for those services.

In their goals, the Cooper/Breaux and Clinton plans are similar – give every American affordable access to quality health care. But, while Clinton proposes to do this through employer mandates, Cooper/Breaux proposes to restructure the insurance system so group policies would be available to all within a designated area at a low, community-based premium.

Cooper/Breaux also lacks the price controls and spending caps in the Clinton plan, while providing broader tax deductions for health care premiums. Cooper/Breaux has been criticized for not guaranteeing universal coverage, just universal *access* to health care. Opponents say the plan would force families to spend far more on health care coverage than they do now, by shifting more of the cost to individuals and away from employers. The Cooper/Breaux plan also limits the states' ability to experiment with different approaches to health care. Critics add that Cooper has not been able to predict the total costs of his plan. Cooper contends that Congress should not try to legislate a cap on health care spending, as it would be asked to do in the White House proposal.

Health Reform Consensus Act

With the Administration's bill foundering and constituents growing impatient for some resolution of the health care debate, both sides of the aisle in Congress are looking for a bipartisan consensus proposal.

There is a growing sentiment in Congress that the time has come to examine practical solutions to some of the most pressing health care coverage issues, such as affordability, portability, renewability and guaranteed issue of health care insurance.

For example, one promising bill, crafted with NFIB's assistance, was introduced in March by Reps. Roy Rowland, D-Ga., and Michael Bilirakis, R-Fla. Additional sponsors of the Health Reform Consensus Act included a bipartisan coalition of 60 other representatives, including key members of the influential House Energy and Commerce Committee, which was scheduled to begin debating health care reform at presstime.

Among the items addressed by this act were:

•Removal of regulatory barriers to small businesses creating insurance purchasing groups. Unlike the White House bill, it does not mandate these groups, but merely loosens present restrictions against them and encourages their use.

•Repeal of state-mandated coverages which dramatically increase the cost of insurance and limit flexibility in writing policies.

•Administrative simplification to reduce paperwork costs, which consumes approximately one-fourth of all health care expenditures.

•100 percent deduction of health insurance for the self-employed. Last year, Congress renewed a 25 percent deduction provision for tax year 1993, but that renewal expired at the end of 1993. At present, there is no deduction for 1994, but Congress is expected either to renew the deduction or incorporate a deduction in a health care reform package.

•Numerous insurance reforms designed to make health care coverage portable, renewable and accessible, to limit preexisting condition exclusions, and to toughen malpractice liability reforms.

Without dictating to small businesses the benefits they must provide to their employees, this bill does say, "Let's do what we can all agree on. Let's try market reforms, let's start bringing down costs and removing restrictions to market reforms, let's reform insurance practices." The consensus bill attempts to find a practical starting point more in the middle of the political spectrum, a point that could begin to offer relief while affording time to solve the more controversial issues.

The Health Equity and Access Today Act

Another proposal that offers small business an alternative to the Administration's plan is the The Health Equity and Access Reform Today Act of 1993, sponsored by Sen. John H. Chafee, R-R.I, and Rep. Bill Thomas, R-Calif.

Similar in many respects to Cooper/Breaux, this act does not rely on employer mandates to pay for health care coverage. Instead, it stresses individual responsibility for health care and provides for a phase-in period when individuals could buy their own coverage. Employers would be required to make insurance plans available but not to pay for them.

The Chafee proposal would allow small businesses and individuals to form voluntary purchasing groups to spread risk and lower premiums. Premiums would be tax-deductible for everyone, but the deduction would be limited to low-cost plans in order to encourage cost-conscious decisions. Age-adjusted community rating replaces experience rating in setting premiums. The act also would pre-empt state-mandated coverages and reform administrative systems and medical liability laws.

Canadian/Single-payer Model

Once a strong contender in the health care debate, a nationalized, single-payer Canadian style plan has lost much of its former support. Although unlikely to re-emerge as a strong contender, the proposal by Rep. Jim McDermott, D-Wash., is still before Congress. In this system, the government is a "monopsony" – a single buyer of all services – responsible for setting budgets, buying and overseeing all health care.

Perhaps because it is our next-door neighbor and yet has such a different system, Canada's approach begets unusually ardent supporters and detractors.

Supporters praise the high degree of reliance on primary and preventive care to try to reduce much more costly curative treatments later. Access is equal and costs, while rising, are lower than here. It is also an easy-to-grasp concept, and this seeming simplicity makes it an attractive alternative to its more complex rivals.

Detractors deride the lack of ready availability of new technologies and treatments. The centralization of state-of-the-art procedures in a few centers tends to promote lengthy waits and long journeys to obtain them. There are also long waits for many standard procedures, and costs are rising rapidly as the population ages, critics say. They also point to the existence of a thriving "black market" of connections through which some Canadians have more equal access than others, and to the large number of Canadians who come south to avoid the wait for care.

In fact, it is hard to compare the American and Canadian systems fairly. The two countries vary widely in total population and demographics. Canada has far fewer urban poor suffering from near-epidemics of poverty-related illnesses and violence. Canada's health care system is based on a much less aggressive treatment philosophy, encouraged in part by budget constraints.

Canada's health care system is funded by heavy national and provincial taxes, which have failed to cover all costs. As a result, care tends to be rationed to stretch budgets. Those most likely to respond best to the most expensive treatments get care first. Others get less aggressive care, or simply wait. When the budgets run out, as they do, services are curtailed.

Although originally envisioned as free to all, the system's rising costs have forced some provinces to introduce patient fees to help stretch budgets further. As Canada struggles to keep its system afloat, the likelihood of its being tried in the States will continue to recede.

Building the Perfect Small Business Health Care System

While small business owners oppose employer mandates, they greatly support many of the reform aspects in the various health care reform plans, including the White House plan. In evaluating the different proposals, the following conditions can serve as a checklist for a nearly "ideal" small business health reform plan:

•Allow formation of health insurance purchasing groups.

•Allow 100 percent tax deduction for health insurance premiums paid by self-employed business owners and by employees.

•Reform insurance industry policies to make coverage easier and less costly to buy, specifically, eliminate preexisting condition and medical exclusion limitations, and guarantee portability and renewability.

•Preempt costly state benefit mandates, which alone can account for an extra 30 percent of premiums.

•Remove state prohibitions against managed care.

•Develop a uniform, affordable, basic standard benefits package, drawing on businesses and consumers for input.

•Reform medical malpractice laws that encourage

defensive medicine and inhibit research and development. Reducing defensive medical practices could alone save $30 billion, according to some estimates.

•Reform the administration of health care. Up to 25 cents of every health care dollar is spent on paperwork. Truly reforming the administrative aspects of health care – simplifying forms, implementing electronic claims filing and processing – would put more money to work in actual care, and help reduce overall expenses.

•Expand the information available to consumers to help them choose more wisely in buying health care. Consumers don't really know what their coverage and care costs. So they have little incentive, or useful information, to help them select efficient, cost-conscious care.

What You Can do to Help Find a Cure

Congressional actions during 1994 could well determine the course of health care for decades. Therefore, we are currently living through one of the most critical periods in the history of small business in America.

What happens in the nation's political arena during 1994 – and the decision of small business owners to get involved or sit this one out on the sidelines – will have a direct impact on every small company's ability to succeed, or even survive, in the future.

President Clinton and his supporters in Congress are going all out to build momentum in support of federal mandates requiring every small business in America to provide health care insurance for all full- and part-time employees and dependents. And as we have seen, not just any health care insurance policy, but platinum-plated Fortune 500-model coverage.

There is no time to waste in the battle against this job-destroying provision of the President's plan.

As we have also seen, on Capitol Hill, there are several less radical solutions which do not lead the nation down the path to direct government control of an additional one-seventh of the nation's economy. Intelligent solutions that will allow employees of small business to obtain affordable and portable insurance coverage.

Nevertheless, the White House continues to turn the heat up on its insistence that small business owners should bear the financial burden for providing "universal coverage" for all American's health care.

But with your immediate help, during the coming days, small business owners can help move Capitol Hill support away from the administration's employer mandate solution and to less radical solutions being worked out in Congress.

How? The health care issue is extremely complex. But this is an election year and lawmakers know their votes on this one issue will help determine-whether many of them return in January 1995. And there will be great pressure for them to act before the November polls.

Small business owners should learn as much as possible about the issue and the different proposals before

Congress. They should talk to their employees and to other small business owners about the issue. And they should try to figure out how the administration's plan will impact their bottom lines.

Then they should forcefully tell their representatives and senators how they feel. Those who support employer mandates are proclaiming their unwavering support for this new government payroll tax.

Now is the time to make your voice heard.

4

Taxes: Government's Idea of Working for a Living

S mall business owners, with much justification, tend to paraphrase the old saw about death and taxes – they say taxes will be the death of them.

So far, the Clinton administration has handed small businesses a mixed bag of tax law changes, most contained in the 1993 Budget Reconciliation Act. An avowed supporter of small businesses – as governor of Arkansas, Clinton received the NFIB's Guardian of Small Business award – Clinton continues to say he wants to help keep the job-creation engine turning.

However, many small business owners see the Administration's employer-mandated health care reform proposal as a potentially devastating tax-and-spend measure (for more on this topic, see Chapter 3). They also eye with distrust Congress' never-ending search for new sources of revenue, and its seeming inability to live within a budget. And they decry Congress' unwillingness to consider true deficit-reduction – i.e., spending reduction – measures.

Meanwhile, business owners say they are spending an increasing amount of time coping with the paperwork created by federal, state and local taxes. This time taken away from business – and family – constitutes an invisible yet real additional tax on businesses, one that is paid through lost business, lost sleep and lost time.

The Budget Reconciliation Act

Small business owners have little reason to be reconciled to 1993's Budget Reconciliation Act. Not only did the act raise tax rates that apply to many small businesses, it also made those changes retroactive to Jan. 1, 1993. For companies with thin profit margins – or no margins at all – retroactivity was a double blow to their business plans.

The majority of U.S. businesses pay taxes as individuals – proprietorships, partnerships and subchapter S corporations. They were encouraged to do so by reductions in personal income tax rates created by the 1986 tax reform act. Most new businesses are unincorporated, as are many small businesses. According to some estimates, subchapter S corporations and sole proprietorships and self-employed persons comprise almost 89 percent of personal tax returns reporting large amounts of business income.

Those business owners now are in a double bind:

•Changes to the tax code in 1993 added two new personal income tax brackets – married couples filing jointly face a 36 percent rate on taxable income above $140,000, as do individuals who earn more than $115,000 in taxable income. The rate increases to 39.6 percent for couples and individuals who have taxable income above $250,000.

These new rates severely impacted small business owners filing as subchapter S corporations, partnerships and sole-proprietorships. The top individual (non-corporate) income tax rate of 36 percent for joint filers with taxable income over $140,000 actually comes out to 38.9 percent for these business owners, when Medicare tax changes are included. The act removed the cap on Medicare taxes, which had been set at the first $135,000 of income. Employees are taxed at 1.45 percent, while the self-employed pay 2.9 percent on all their income.

If the business owner makes more than $250,000 in a given year, a so-called "millionaire surtax" of 10 percent takes effect, raising the effective tax rate to 42.5 percent.

For individuals who earn more than $108,450, the tax law limits deductibility of itemized deductions. This generates an additional 1 percent effective tax rate, bringing the top brackets to 39.9 percent or 43.5 percent for millionaires.

•Such drastic increases in the effective tax rates could tempt many business owners to seek to file under the corporate rates, which takes time, money, lawyers and accountants. If they do, they could be double-taxed – required to pay taxes on their income both as companies and also as a recipients of dividends or capital gains.

The 1993 tax law also reduced business-related meal expense deductions from 80 percent of the tab to 50 percent and removed the business-expense deduction for club memberships. It also increased taxes on gasoline and diesel fuel.

There were some bright notes, however:

•The new law did allow people facing unexpectedly higher taxes because of the new retroactive brackets to pay the additional taxes in three equal installments due in April of 1994, 1995 and 1996, without interest.

•The expensing limit on business equipment was raised from $10,000 to $17,500.

•For the self-employed, the tax act retroactively extended a 25 percent deduction for their medical insurance premiums. The deduction had expired July 1, 1992. While not giving the full deductibility that larger businesses enjoy, it did give some relief by reviving the deduction.

•Individuals who made charitable contributions as a tax-preference item in determining their alternative minimum tax may be eligible for refunds. The law was changed to retroactively allow them to deduct the current value. Previously, they could deduct only the purchase price of the property donated.

•And, if any small business owners had money left over to buy luxury items such as jewelry, boats or planes, they could be due a refund as the 10 percent luxury tax was repealed retroactively.

Endangered Species:
Independent Contractors

Meanwhile, the IRS, the Clinton health care reform plan, many of America's self-employed, and the fate of a number of businesses both small and large seem to be on a collision course.

The point of impact lies in the definition of independent contractor. At issue is who is responsible for paying billions in tax revenue, and possibly billions more for the health care premiums proposed in the Administration's health care reform package. Buried in that proposal is the equivalent of a smart bomb that could decide the issue in the government's favor.

For years, the IRS has doggedly tried to reclassify independent contractors as employees of the businesses with which these self-employed individuals work. Self-employed people pay taxes on what they earn directly to the IRS; if they are employees, then the business is responsible not only for remitting withheld payroll taxes, but also half of Social Security taxes, as well as unemployment tax.

The Clinton Administration's proposed health care reform package raises the stakes by giving the IRS unilateral authority to reclassify many, if not all, independent contractors as part-time employees. Under the health care proposal, employers would be required to pay a portion of the mandatory health insurance premium for part-time workers. The proposed plan would reclassify many independent contractors not only for health care purposes, but for all purposes.

The IRS has said that it believes more than 3 million people who claim to be independent contractors should actually be carried as employees on businesses' books – many of them small companies. For many small and medium-size businesses that rely heavily on independent contractors, reclassification for taxes alone would be a heavy blow; adding in health care could be ruinous.

Compliance Taxes Business Owners' Resources

Most small business owners have at one time or another uttered a short, bitter laugh at the notice printed on most federal forms, advising that they conform to the federal Paperwork Reduction Act. If this is reduction, they think, spare us from the full load.

Complying with the IRS's labyrinthine regulations gives small business owners nightmares, since they usually don't have accounting staff dedicated solely to this task. And it's a nightmare without waking – weekly or biweekly payments of Social Security and withholding taxes, quarterly estimated income tax payments and payroll reports, annual income tax, and constant filing of dozens of other forms, reports and statements related to taxes, citizenship and other business information. And that doesn't include the welter of state and local tax forms.

All this paperwork takes lots of time, time that could be spent on sales, on business planning, on training employees. It also takes money for outside professional accounting help. In hard and soft dollars, complying with the IRS – not counting the actual check – costs at least $123.4 billion, according to The Tax Foundation, a Washington, D.C., research organization supported by corporations.

The IRS itself estimates that a business with $1 million in annual sales will spend at least $5.03 in compliance on every $1,000 in sales, or $5,030. The Tax Foundation has estimated that small businesses spend three to four dollars on compliance for every tax dollar the IRS collects. Others say the cost is actually far higher, if one includes business opportunities that could not be pursued because of resources that went into compliance. In effect, it costs small business more, compared to revenue, to struggle to comply with tax codes than it costs larger businesses.

The 1986 "simplification" of the tax code actually made the situation more complex, tax experts say. This major revision was one of 10 sweeping changes since 1981, including the Clinton Administration's budget bill. Comprising 9,371 amendments to the IRS code, the collective effect of these changes has been to create a maze that confounds even tax professionals.

Even more vexing, legislative changes are only the beginning. The IRS must study Congress' actions before it issues its own regulations which may or may not be Congress' intent. This can take months or years, and frequently results in challenges that cause further revisions.

The outlook for true simplification is not bright. On hold while Congress grapples with health care is a bill sponsored by Rep. Dan Rostenkowski, D-Ill., chairman of the House Ways and Means Committee, which must also deal with health care. This bill would attempt to simplify tax requirements for large partnerships and subchapter S corporations.

Others propose to spell tax relief V-A-T – value added tax. Sen. David L. Boren, D-Okla., and Sen. John Danforth, R-Mo., have been promoting a national sales tax that would eliminate the corporate income tax, reduce payroll taxes, give individual taxpayers a bigger standard deduction, and tax business transactions at a single rate. Although VATs are common in many industrialized nations, they could create new headaches for small businesses, as detailed below.

VAT Doesn't Spell Tax Relief for Small Business

The Clinton Administration's quest to fund its health care reform package has stirred up a decades-old debate – should the United States impose some kind of consumption tax, usually called a value-added tax or VAT, to replace or supplement the income tax.

Currently, the White House has not proposed a VAT to finance health care. The administration floated the idea, but pulled it due to the public outcry against it. However, the tax's potential as a money machine to support big-spending programs continues to tempt the unwary.

A 1993 NFIB survey of small business owners showed that 82 percent opposed using a VAT to pay for health care reform. A similar survey in 1986 indicated that 59 percent opposed replacing the then-current tax system with a VAT. The results were more mixed when owners were asked if they would replace the federal income tax with a consumption tax that encouraged savings and investment – 44 percent opposed, 36 percent favored and 7 percent were undecided.

The lack of public support will not deter either party from talking about VAT a lot in the next few years, predict observers, who say someday the stars may come into line, and small businesses will become all too familiar with the VAT. If there's one constant in Washington, it's a desire for money. Legislators want to return to their districts able to claim they have done something. Unfortunately, whatever they do will likely cost money, no matter whether they're conservative, moderate or liberal. So anything that raises large amounts of money is very attractive, and a VAT is a real money machine.

VAT has been touted by some as a replacement for corporate taxes and payroll taxes, because, in theory, it taxes consumption while encouraging personal saving and business investment. Many who oppose a VAT do so because it can be regressive in nature. For the poorest families and many elderly, who must spend most or all of their income, virtually all of their income would be subject to a VAT. Middle- and upper-income groups who save more would pay proportionately less in taxes.

The United States, Switzerland and Australia are the only three Western nations that don't use a VAT. The issue has been discussed here since World War II, but has failed to arouse much support. One of the strongest arguments against it has been the cost of administering the tax – and the fact that businesses would have to collect the tax and maintain extensive records for the government.

A prime example of an indirect consumption tax (so-called because businesses, not government, actually collect it), the VAT is levied and collected at every stage of manufacture and distribution of goods.

In most European nations that use a VAT, businesses get credits on purchases for taxes paid at previous stages of production and distribution. Each business then pays a tax only on its own markup. As a result, businesses must maintain extensive, long-term record-keeping and record storage. Thanks to political compromises, most countries have built -in exemptions and differing rates of VAT for various goods and services. So the business owner's task becomes more complex in factoring in these exemptions and multiple tax rates.

The result? A record-keeping nightmare for businesses, especially small ones that cannot afford accounting staff. A 1990 survey for NFIB indicated that in Great Britain, companies with under 15 employees used 2.5 percent of their operating costs to comply with the VAT. Larger companies, up to 500 employees, expended only .07 percent of operating costs on compliance.

In Japan, businesses subtract their total year's purchases from total sales, and multiply the remainder by a set figure to determine the tax. This sounds simple as long as the tax rate is uniform and there are no exemptions. Japan does have a uniform (3 percent) rate, with exemptions for very small businesses, but it, too, is looking at multiple rates.

In an ideal world, its proponents say, a VAT would replace income or payroll taxes, and there would be a uniform tax rate, with no exemptions. In the real world, however, countries with VATs have several rates – a high one for luxury items, lower for more mundane purchases – and usually exemptions for necessities such as food and shelter. And no country has replaced its income tax with a VAT. Proponents and critics agree such real-world compromises would be necessary in order to pass a VAT in the United States.

Nevertheless, proponents of a VAT will continue to seek support. They say it would:

•Improve the foreign trade balance because it exempts exports but taxes imports.

•Encourage savings because it does not tax earnings on savings and investments.

•Stimulate business.

•Help reduce the deficit.

In addition to the burden collecting a VAT would place on small businesses, opponents cite the following:

•Remote likelihood that VAT will replace income tax, so it would not stimulate the economy or savings,

but would foster further government spending.
- •Regressive nature of VAT.
- •Heavy administrative costs.
- •Potential to increase inflation.
- •Infringement on state governments' taxing powers.
- •Potential for fraud and evasion.

Meanwhile, two proposals – the "Simplified Alternative Tax" and the "Savings Exempt Income Tax" – have been made for a direct consumption tax, that is, a tax paid straight to the government. These taxes would be levied, essentially, on the difference between what you save or invest and your total earnings. Neither idea has been introduced as legislation, however.

Balanced Budget Amendment:
Seeking an Unhappy Medium

With the federal deficit for 1994 pegged at $223 billion, Congress once again took up debate over a balanced budget amendment to the Constitution. In March, Congress turned down a balanced budget proposal, which based part of its balancing power on tax hikes. Cynical observers noted this kind of legislative election-year maneuvering allows lawmakers to report home that they voted in favor of a popular (but doomed) bill, while actually failing to take real steps toward deficit reduction.

Some of the steps the proposed legislation included:
- •Means testing for all entitlement programs, including

Social Security. In essence, wealthier retirees who have outside income from investments or savings would receive less, little or no Social Security. If their financial situations change, they would become eligible.

•Closing some under-utilized veterans' hospitals.

•Grounding the proposed space station.

•Raising the retirement age to 68, thus generating additional tax revenue from extra years of work by the rapidly growing senior population, and creating savings from postponed Social Security payouts.

Over the past 15 years, the federal deficit has grown from $700 billion to $3.5 trillion. This staggering debt restricts access by businesses to capital. It also threatens to hold future generations hostage to our profligate ways.

Nevertheless, despite countless speeches condemning the deficit, Congress has seemed unable to impose the kind of self-discipline small business owners practice every day. Neither of the two incarnations of Gramm-Rudman-Hollings nor a number of agreements between administrations and Congress have succeeded in instilling self-discipline. As Sen. Paul Simon, D-Ill., the sponsor of the balanced budget bill, has been quoted as saying, "We need the discipline of a constitutional amendment to force us to face fiscal realities."

But do they really need to amend the Constitution to receive that discipline? Not if Congress really wanted to reduce the deficit. Legislation proposed in 1993 by the bipartisan House team of Reps. Tim Penny, D-Minn., and John Kasich, R-Ohio, proposed widely spread spending cuts that could have reduced the deficit by some $103 billion in five years. The 80 spending reductions included cutting $50 billion from entitlements, $26 billion from non-mandatory spending, and $27 billion from personnel costs. The measure was defeated.

Even a constitutional amendment doesn't guarantee an end to over-spending. All the states except Vermont permit certain spending programs to be outside the budget. The Clinton administration has already teed off in this game by attempting to place its health care reform costs outside the budget – by calling the mandatory payments that employers would make for employee health insurance coverage "premiums" instead of "taxes."

It has been estimated that spending would have to be cut by $600 billion over five years in order to hit the zero-deficit bull's eye. The balanced budget legislation that was taken up by the Senate in late February did not permit capital spending outside the budget, although it does have an emergency relief valve for helping victims of catastrophes such as the Los Angeles earthquake.

A constitutional amendment must receive a two-thirds vote by Congress and ratification by at least 38 states. So, even if Congress gets around to a balanced budget amendment this year, its future would be highly uncertain.

Small business owners have indicated in numerous NFIB surveys they support deficit reduction through cutting spending, not by imposing new taxes or extending existing ones. Amending the Constitution is not, and was not intended to be, easy. A faster, more efficient way to achieve deficit reduction is to support brave candidates for House and Senate who will work for spending cuts.

Profit-sharing Plans, Estate Taxes Under Attack:

Profit-sharing

You can't take it with you and, if some inside the Beltway have their say, you can't have it before you go, either.

For many small businesses, age- and service-weighted profit sharing plans provide efficient, flexible ways to offer retirement benefits to loyal employees. But, the U.S. Department of Labor wants to outlaw new weighted plans starting this year and eliminate all weighted plans by 1997.

The Department of Labor's proposal is part of the administration's Pension Benefit Guaranty Corporation reform package. The government argues that these plans could be used to reward older employees – especially the principals and top management – at the expense of lower ranking employees.

While the possibility of abuse always exists, these plans have been around for decades and have repeatedly satisfied nondiscrimination requirements of the IRS and other watchdogs. Existing regulations provide ample protection against the kind of abuse that worries the Labor Department.

Profit sharing encourages employees to take a greater

interest in the success of the business – to be more efficient, productive and loyal. For most small businesses, weighted profit sharing plans allow owners to reward employees who stuck through lean years while the business became profitable. Often, profit sharing may be the only way a small business can provide retirement benefits for the owner and for other long-time employees.

According to a survey by the Profit Sharing Council of America, an industry group, small companies that do not offer retirement plans now would have even less reason to do so in the future, if they could not tailor them to meet employees' needs and situations.

About 25 percent of NFIB members have pension plans of some kind. Profit sharing plans, in particular, are ideal from the standpoint of a small business owner who has worked hard for years to build a business and has only a limited number of years to retirement. It usually takes years before a small business is profitable enough so the owner can start and contribute meaningfully to a retirement plan. These plans allow the owner the flexibility of accelerated funding for older employees – usually the owner – to catch up for those lean years, as well as rewarding loyal, productive employees who come in later.

Unfortunately, there are those who think that contributions for a brand-new employee should be as high as those for principals and workers who have given years to building up an enterprise.

Estate Taxes

Under the 1993 tax law changes, the top rates for estate taxes have risen from 50 percent to 53 percent on estates of $2.5 million to $3 million, and 55 percent for estates over $3 million.

When the owner of a family business or farm dies, the value of the operation becomes part of the total estate. It's not unusual for low-profit enterprises to have surprisingly high paper values – farms are but one example – and thus to be exposed to confiscatorily high taxes. Although a large life insurance policy might help defray those taxes, the premiums for sufficient coverage are frequently too high for the business owner to absorb.

All too often, the enterprise must be sold to pay taxes, leaving little or nothing for the heirs who had hoped to carry it on. In fact, only 7 percent of family businesses remain intact past two generations.

Currently, estate taxes are graduated, with the first $600,000 exempted from taxation. But the next $150,000 is taxed at 37 percent and, as indicated above, the rates climb to 55 percent. For example, the taxes on a $1 million estate are $345,800, or an effective tax rate of 34.5 percent. Small businesses are allowed to spread out payments over a number of years, but that can still drain off scarce resources needed for expansion – or survival.

Then President-elect Bill Clinton scared many small and family business owners before his inauguration when he said he might consider taxing capital gains on the value of property at the time of the owner's death.

Presently, capital gains taxes apply to appreciation of property starting from the time of the owner's death. Clinton's suggestion was part of the Tax Reform Act of 1976, but its implementation was delayed and the provision finally repealed after considerable NFIB opposition. So far, as president, Clinton has not revisited this change to capital gains laws.

Happily, some in Congress want to bring small business owners some relief. Rep. Bill Brewster, D-Okla., has said he hopes to introduce a bill that would allow heirs to defer estate taxes on businesses valued below an as-yet undetermined level until the enterprises are sold outside the family. These businesses must comprise at least 40 percent of the decedent's estate and have heirs who were actively involved in the operation of the business for at least eight month's before the owner's death. Sen. John Breaux, R-La., introduced similar legislation in the 102nd Congress and may do so again this year.

The family's ownership would end when 40 percent or more of the enterprise is sold to someone outside the family; or 60 percent or more is sold to a family member who is not an heir; or a non-family member has been in control of the business for more than 270 days.

Critics are expected to argue that this proposal would be simply a loophole or small business favor designed to deprive the government of tax revenue. In fact, while deferring the actual payment of the tax, the bill would help generate revenue by providing employment and generating business.

5

You Put Up the Money; I'll Tell You How To Run It: Government Intrusion into the Workplace

I t must be one of the greatest ironies of this decade. Powerful voices within the U.S. government are calling for increasing the role of government in the American workplace to a more "European" style of business that mandates higher employee wages and benefits – at the same time that Europe is foundering in the highest unemployment it has experienced in modern times. Yet no one in government has paused to ask, "Why would we want to imitate an economic system that has created no net new jobs in 15 years?"

Government got involved in business originally to protect workers from exploitation, unsafe workplaces and the sweatshop conditions that were rampant during the darkest days of the Industrial Revolution. We all agree that such abhorrent conditions are to be condemned. But we are not so naive as to believe that government's role in the workplace has not gone far beyond that of protecting the safety of workers or prohibiting exploitation.

Today, the government takes an active role in prescribing the wages a company must pay its workers, the benefits it must offer, even the most subtle details of employer-employee relations. The increased role of government – which began with the noblest of intentions – now does little other than create regulations and paperwork, which result only in slower company growth, fewer people employed and more closed businesses. Each and every regulation and mandated benefit serve only to increase the cost of labor. Let's call it what it is: a tax on jobs. And, there's considerable likelihood those in Washington will try to raise that invisible tax.

Want proof? Take a closer look at Europe's situation. The countries on the Continent mandate an extremely rich set of benefits, minimum wages and payroll taxes, which account for nearly half of a company's total labor costs. The result as we stated earlier: no jobs. Europe has created no net new jobs in the past 20 years. In addition, most of the jobs that have been created are government jobs, not private employment. Europe's unemployment rate is nearly twice that of the United States.

You see how easy it is for government to significantly hinder the job creation process, yet government can do little to spur job creation. Politicians forget, ignore or fail to understand how severely their actions impact small businesses' ability to generate jobs. And it is small businesses that are most sensitive to government intrusion, for two good reasons. First, small business owners are the least likely to exploit their employees – because they personally know each one. And second, small business owners do not

have the time or money to keep up with the rules and regulations that seem to change on every bureaucrat's whim.

Not Just Employees, Friends

While it is common for executives of a large corporation never to meet or know the names of the vast majority
of their employees, most small business owners are on a
first-name basis with theirs. They talk every day, not only
about business but about spouses and children, birthdays
and graduations, good times and bad. Small business
owners are not isolated from their employees, blindly issuing orders from some executive suite. They work, often
side by side with employees, to make the business successful for everyone's benefit.

When this kind of personal relationship exists, human
nature dictates that there is little chance for employee
exploitation – indeed, just the opposite is true. Typically,
small business owners are more democratic in their decision making. They work things out with their employees,
often on an individual basis, creating flexible work hours,
leave policies, benefits packages, compensation arrangements and working conditions that fit employees' needs.
Unfortunately, that flexibility may soon come to an end.
The government, through its misguided efforts to protect
workers, is destroying this relationship with an increasing
number of rules, regulations and mandates.

For example, small business owners who employ more

than 50 people may not confer with employees to establish a mutually agreeable leave policy or even a contingency plan for an individual employee with a special situation. Even if the employees themselves would rather have a stricter leave policy in exchange for other benefits, it's no deal. Rather, the government dictates a one-size-fits-all leave policy for all companies that size. In short, government is depersonalizing the relationship between small business employers and employees, making it more like the adversarial big business/big labor relationship.

The Compliance Trap

Big business also has the advantage of financial resources when it comes to regulatory compliance. They can hire legal eagles to explain (if not get around) the ever-changing bureaucratic interpretations of the broad rules government enacts. Sadly, small businesses are too often found to be in violation of these broad rules, usually due to a bad apple or two. Despite their best efforts to be in compliance, they often lack the necessary legal resources to catch everything. In fact, the overwhelming number of infractions are paperwork errors – failing to fill out or improperly filling out the rising tide of government forms that washes over the small business owner's desk on a daily basis.

This administrative burden keeps the small business owner from focusing on the task at hand – running the business and, it is hoped, turning a profit. It is, after all, the owner's reputation – and, typically, personal savings – that are on the line. Besides not having legal staff, small businesses don't have the administrative personnel to help complete the paperwork. It is most often the owner who must wade through the confusing regulations and fill out the paperwork as accurately as possible. This is time that could be spent making more sales, turning out more product or improving employee relations.

But getting it wrong can cost a small business thousands of dollars. For example, a small business in Louisiana was growing rapidly, with orders piling up. The employees were working 50 hours a week to keep up with demand. Instead of paying the workers the minimum wage for 40 hours and time-and-a-half for the remaining 10, the owner paid more than the time-and-a-half rate for all 50 hours. With the business rush, and since the pay exceeded what was required by law, the owner did not keep accurate records of overtime hours worked. What did he get for his generosity? A $12,000 fine from the Department of Labor.

The owner of a day care center in Virginia also found himself overwhelmed with OSHA regulations. The owner operated a clean facility and tried to comply with the letter of the law, but found some of OSHA's requirements extreme. For example, in the 134-page manual detailing requirements in dealing with blood-borne pathogens, mucus and blood are defined as hazardous materials. If a child scrapes her elbow or has a runny nose, the staff person must put on gloves before attending to the youth. Diapers are also hazardous and require special disposal. Any infraction is punishable by a minimum fine of $7,000. In addition, the business must keep extensive records and maintain them for 30 years. Does anyone find it a little extreme that children could grow up and have children of their own before their former day care center was allowed to throw away its records?

Of course, the cost of compliance is nothing compared to the cost of a possible investigation, whether warranted or not. Business owners large and small know of disgruntled employees filing frivolous lawsuits or falsified complaints with the Equal Employment Opportunity Commission. Either way, the employer's lawyer will frequently advise settling the case, because it would cost more to prove the company's innocence.

The EEOC isn't the only place disgruntled employees go to cause employers harm. A manufacturing company in Ohio found itself under investigation by OSHA and the EPA after it fired an employee for poor performance. The employee chose to get even by falsely accusing the company of violating regulations. As a result, OSHA conducted three inspections and interviewed all employees, most of them on company time. A fourth OSHA inspection revisited the claims made by the employee. While the company was cleared of all charges, the inspector found three unrelated violations – not safety violations, but incomplete written procedures – which cost the company $825 in fines. The EPA investigation took nearly six weeks and found nothing. The company lost thousands of dollars in legal fees and downtime, with no recourse except the satisfaction that its tax dollars funded the investigations.

These examples are typical of the experiences most businesses have had with government agencies, yet government involvement in the workplace continues to grow.

Family Leave

The Family and Medical Leave Act, which became effective in August 1993, is one of the most recent examples of government telling employers how to run their businesses. It is also an example of an expensive, government-mandated benefit that will ultimately cost some people their jobs. In fact, much of the justification for the law was that most industrialized countries (read European countries) have such a benefit. And, as discussed above, this law and benefits like it have cost Europe any new job growth over the past 20 years.

The Family and Medical Leave Act requires an employer to grant an employee, in certain family situations including the birth of a child or death of a loved one, up to 12 weeks of unpaid leave with no loss in seniority or job responsibility. Thankfully, NFIB was able to secure a small business exemption from this regulation for businesses with fewer than 50 employees. Companies of that size cannot afford to lose a team member for three months with no other recourse. The law offers a good example of how well-intentioned politicians are constantly expanding government's role in business.

Like many government mandates, this law was driven more by political motivations than by an expressed need on the part of workers. In 1991, a study by Peen-Shoen/Concerned Alliance of Responsible Employers found that 89 percent of employees preferred to have benefits negotiated between the employer and employee, not imposed by a government mandate. Also, in a 1990 Gallup/Employee Benefit Research Institute poll, only 1 percent of respondents considered family leave the most important employer-provided benefit, while 16 percent named it the least important. Despite these statistics, the government enacted the mandated benefit that, like all mandated benefits, results in lower pay and fewer jobs.

And like many government prescribed benefits, the Family and Medical Leave Act is not a simple law. The act required more than 90 pages of regulations drawn up by agency bureaucrats to interpret it. Now, business owners must spend more time and money to accurately translate the regulations to the workplace or risk being fined for noncompliance.

Labor Law Reform

The same well-intentioned government officials are now discussing the future of the workplace. As part of this discussion, they are considering significant changes to the relationship between employer and employee. Of course, the "solution" is increased government involvement.

U.S. Secretary of Labor Robert Reich's Labor Law Reform Commission, composed mostly of representatives from organized labor, academia and big business, has the intended goal of restoring a "level playing field" to labor/management relations. While its full report has not been released at this writing, it is a safe bet that the panel will try to bring about a significant increase in government's role in the workplace and create a more adversarial relationship between government and employers. Besides significant changes to the National Labor Relations Act, the commission is recommending several changes in employer-employee relations that could fundamentally affect business' ability to create jobs.

Though the government's goal is supposed to be improving the plight of the worker through management of employer-employee relations, the so-called "solutions" put forth by government officials are actually hurting workers by impeding job creation. Among the issues soon to be addressed are worker training, minimum wage, child labor, striker replacement, right-to-work laws and OSHA reform.

Worker Training

Small businesses are labor-intensive, so employee productivity is paramount to each business' success.

101

Overwhelmingly, small business owners provide some form of on-the-job training, often conducting it internally on an informal basis. Obviously, a small business owner is not going to hire someone to perform a task without making sure the person can adequately do so. Since the training is on a more personal, informal level, the time and expense is rarely tracked or documented. Yet, the result is the same – more skilled and more productive employees. As a company grows, the employees grow with it, by taking on more responsibility and learning new tasks.

Some within the government want a formal system, to be funded by a payroll tax, mandated expenditure or some other measure. Forcing business owners to provide formalized training to their employees may improve the skill base of the work force (just as the informal method did), but at the cost of job growth.

Employers, faced with the expense of a formal training program and the paperwork that will accompany it, would need to cut costs somewhere else to pay for it all. Margins are already thin at most businesses, and since the increased costs are personnel related, the cuts would come from the same area in the form of lower wages or fewer employees.

Minimum Wage

As the largest employers of minimum wage earners, small businesses are extremely sensitive to any changes in the minimum wage. Most observers on Capitol Hill believe Congress will probably consider an increase in the minimum wage before 1995. What is driving this move? Overwhelmingly, it is organized labor acting in concert with congressional liberals who believe they will help the working poor. They will argue that no one could support a family on the current minimum wage and that a raise is long since due.

However, demographic studies show that minimum wage earners are not necessarily the working poor. Very few, about 10 percent, in fact, are year-round workers who are the sole supporters of a family. According to the Bureau of Labor Statistics, about one-third of minimum wage earners are teenagers. Another half are employed part-time, and many of those are single and live in a home with a relative as the head of the household.

The costs related to a minimum wage increase are many: unemployment insurance premiums, workers' compensation premiums, Social Security and disability benefit costs. The bottom line is that a minimum wage increase will hurt those it is intended to help. Only a small percentage of workers will benefit, while the majority of employers in the country will be forced to freeze hiring or lay off employees to pay for the increased labor costs.

Child Labor

State child labor laws vary and are more specific

regarding local industries, but in general, they are more restrictive than federal laws. There are many benefits for teenagers who work, as long as they are protected from potentially harmful job situations. Local and state laws are best equipped to do this.

Creating an additional layer of federal laws and permits will, in most cases, add nothing and harm the employment environment for teenagers and small businesses. As the government increases (and duplicates) child labor regulations, small business owners will find it too complicated and too risky to hire teens. And while that is bad for business, it is far worse for the responsible young people who need or want jobs.

Striker Replacement

At this writing, striker replacement legislation is currently stalled in the U.S. Senate. Having passed the House of Representatives, S. 55 does not have the support necessary to bring it up for consideration in the Senate. Even though the unions do not have the vote necessary to break a filibuster, they insist on bringing it up to see if they can arm twist two senators to vote their way. This would virtually guarantee passage of the bill. Given this, small business owners must continue to let their senators know how detrimental striker replacement legislation would be to their businesses.

In 1992, the legislation met a similar fate. But organized

labor considers this legislation top priority, so you can bet it will keep coming back. The bill would have amended the National Labor Relations Act to make it an unfair labor practice to permanently replace workers who walk off the job in an economic strike (one over issues like pay, hours and benefits) or to give employment preference to workers who cross picket lines. Business owners believe that employers must have the right to keep their business operating through a strike by hiring permanent replacements, just as workers have the right to strike. To eliminate that balance would skew labor relations to the unions' advantage and drive many companies, large and small, out of business.

Right-to-Work

It's a strange thing, how the federal government tends to insulate itself from the direct impact of its actions, by exempting itself from the laws it passes. For example, congressional liberals are seeking to tear down state right-to-work statutes at the same time federal employees enjoy right-to-work protection. These laws prevent membership or non-membership in a labor union from being a condition for employing an individual. Twenty states have explicit right-to-work laws, and more than 30 have protections for at least some public employees. This pro-business environment encourages new businesses to locate in a state and existing businesses to expand – creating jobs that benefit the whole economy of the state. Weakening these laws harms the business environment, and endangers the survival of small and new companies.

OSHA Reform

The defeat of a comprehensive OSHA reform bill in 1992 slowed, but did not stop, organized labor's push for dramatic changes to OSHA guidelines. The proposed "reforms" are expected to resurface in the labor-friendlier atmosphere of the current Congress and administration. These include management-employee relations (on which Labor Secretary Reich has already held hearings), creation of safety committees, expansion of criminal penalties for noncompliance, and a host of other regulations and paperwork requirements.

Worker safety committees cost businesses thousands of dollars in unproductive time and associated paperwork, a cost that is not recouped by any overhead savings generated by the committees. They render a company uncompetitive, leading to lower wages or layoffs, and foster an adversarial work environment. In addition, some believe these committees could be considered bargaining units by the National Labor Relations Board. If this is the case, enacting this bill could invite union organizing in companies required to comply.

And expanding criminal penalties to those who do not comply is not the answer. Under current law, if an employee is killed on the job and the accident is determined to be the fault of the employer, the employer may be criminally liable. All agree that this is fair. However, under the proposed OSHA reform bill, the employer may be criminally liable if an employee suffers "serious bodily injury" resulting from a "willful violation" of company safety regulations. The penalties are bad enough, but the vague terms could open the floodgates to meritless lawsuits. Defending against these lawsuits will put many small businesses out of business.

That is, if the paperwork nightmare of the expanded OSHA regulations doesn't put them out of business first. The OSHA reform bill requires all businesses – no exceptions – to create written safety and health programs. These detailed documents must include extensive explanations of methods and procedures for identifying safety and health hazards, as well as procedures for providing safety and health training. For small businesses that may never have dealt with OSHA before, this would create an enormous paperwork load, meaning an enormous time and financial burden. The result: higher costs of doing business, fewer jobs and no overall increase in worker safety.

Turn the Tables: Tell Congress How to Run Government

Fortunately, although the climate in Washington is more sympathetic to labor than it has been for some time, many of the above actions are still pending. And, in an election year tinged by voter unrest and the hint of scandal, Congress will move cautiously on major legislation. There is still time to make your opinions heard on OSHA, minimum wage laws, right-to-work, child labor, striker replacement and worker training. Contact your lawmakers. Tell them how government intrusions make it more difficult for you to create jobs in your community. Offer to testify before committees about how this government tinkering will affect your business. Don't allow the failed European employment model to become the norm in this country.

6

Protecting the Environment, But Who Will Protect Small Business?

H ide the cedar chest, grandma. The EPA's a-comin'! Yes, one of the more recent signs that environmental regulations have gotten insanely out of control was reported last year in *The Wall Street Journal* (and we assure you we did not make this up):

> "Acting under the Federal Insecticide, Fungicide and Rodenticide Act, the EPA is demanding that Seventh Generation Inc., a small 'green' catalog retailer, register as a pesticide the cedar blocks it sells to repel moths. 'Moths hate the fresh woody scent,' the catalog declares. The EPA, acting on a tip from a state agricultural inspector, asserts that the small Colchester, Vt., company violates environmental rules by making 'pesticidal claims' for the cedar blocks."

Wood chips. Yes, this is wood chips we're talking about, folks. The whole thing sounds like a bad comedy sketch you'd see on "Saturday Night Live." You can almost imagine this anonymous state agricultural inspector, wearing trench coat, fedora and dark glasses, whispering into a pay phone. "Yep, this cedar stuff sounds highly volatile. You better get up here fast."

It gets worse. Not only were the cedar blocks not registered as a pesticide (Oh, the horror!), the product violated regulations in other areas: no list of ingredients, no listing of the product's toxicity and inadequate directions for use. (Honest, we're really not making this up.)

Can you imagine how this company will comply with these regulations? "This block of wood contains: wood. That's it. Just wood. It's not toxic, but if you feel compelled to try and choke it down, you'll have more fiber in your system than your colon could probably handle in a week. Directions for use: Open drawer. Place block of wood in drawer. Close drawer. What are you, stupid?"

The story would be pretty funny, if it weren't so tragic. Think of the money this company must now spend on permits, lawyers, repackaging and wasted time to register, of all things, blocks of wood. What next? Fly-swatters? Cowboy boots? Better register those pointy-toed, two-steppin' roach stompers now, or they'll throw you sock-footed in the slammer. ("What're ya in for, Slim?" "Bug squashin' without a license. You?" "They got me for running an illegal wood chip ring and laundering the funds through my brother-in-law's Christmas tree farm.")

All joking aside, this ludicrous (but sadly, true) story, is just another reminder of the stranglehold the federal government has placed on small business, under the guise of protecting the environment. Once these misguided, but well-intended, laws get into the hands of overzealous bureaucratic regulators, they are twisted into an unrecognizable mess, with which it is impossible to comply.

Of course, it is the inability to comply that regulators rely on. Too many seem to take the attitude that there is no way anyone could comply with so many regulations – least of all a small company that can't afford a lawyer to even decipher the regulations. So they keep looking until they find something, anything, and then turn a handy profit in fines. (Do we sound cynical? Read on.)

B&E, Inc., an oil field saltwater disposal company in Carlsbad, N.M., obtained permits in 1982 to legally discharge produced water in Laguna Quatro, a salt water playa (basin), according to an article written in the *Oil & Gas Journal*, July 5, 1993. The permits were approved by the New Mexico Oil Conservation Division (OCD) and the U.S. Bureau of Land Management. Then, according to the article, in 1991, some years after the approval, the EPA decided to review saltwater disposal practices in the state. (Here it comes.)

The EPA fined 38 oil producers in five states that had used B&E's services. The fines, however, were dropped due to pressure from legislators and even environmentalists outraged by the inconclusiveness of the EPA's findings.

B&E, which cooperated fully with the investigation, was fined more than $4 million, despite an obvious lack of credible evidence that the produced water harmed salt playas. The OCD director was quoted in the article saying,

"They [EPA officials] did not seem to look into the possibility there is a naturally occurring salt."

Yet all the fines against B&E were not dropped. And the company, to avoid an expensive drawn-out lawsuit, ended up agreeing to pay a "smaller" ($25,000) fine to the government, for something it had state and federal permission to do in the first place.

These examples, admittedly extreme, are offered simply to prove a point: regulatory interference in nature, as in business, just doesn't work. Environmental regulations have gotten way out of hand and must be brought under some form of logical control.

Unfortunately, however, with the legislation expected to be addressed in Congress this session, small business owners can expect only more "green tape" – stringent environmental regulations that will send administrative costs skyrocketing for small businesses and for state and federal governments. The results: more small business closings, more government waste and little progress on real environmental protection.

Small business owners should pay particular attention to new environmental legislation. Superfund reform and reauthorization of the Clean Water Act are the two most pressing environmental issues expected to be addressed by Congress during 1994.

The concerns of small businesses regarding private property rights and just compensation are ongoing. They are affected by current regulations associated with the Endangered Species Act (ESA), wetlands reform, and the

Resource Conservation and Recovery Act (RCRA). While those issues may or may not be addressed during the 103rd Congress, small business owners should keep informed in order to effectively argue against harmful regulations.

If small business owners were considered a separate species – and many would argue that they ought to be seen just that way – they would appear on every endangered list around. Given the generally hazardous environment small businesses are born into, the legislative toxins that pervade their habitat, and the 50-percent-plus die-off rate for young companies, Congress would be rushing to help them. Instead, lawmakers seem bent on testing the limits of this unique breed's endurance – and there isn't much relief in sight.

Superfund

The reauthorization of Superfund, the nation's primary hazardous waste cleanup law, will be a congressional priority in 1994. It is a priority for small business owners as well. Too many have been roped into the litigation web by being named in third-party lawsuits by larger polluters, in their effort to slow down the litigation process and spread the financial liability. These small business owners are then forced to spend thousands of dollars defending themselves for actions they knew nothing about.

Take, for example, the case of Merle Hahn, who owns

Gamble's Hardware Store in Lusk, Wyo. In 1986, Hahn sold some junk batteries to a man who illegally disposed of the acid by pouring it on the ground outside his shop. Because of that $13.50 sale, Hahn became one of 54 companies that were named as third-party defendants in the Superfund cleanup of the site, estimated to cost $1.2 million. Hahn and the other defendants were forced to settle out of court for $10,000 each. "It was as if I had sold some shells to a guy who then went out and shot somebody, and they come and blame me for the murder," Hahn said. "It is ridiculous."

The average life span of these third-party lawsuits is three to six years, and the money spent typically winds up in the pockets of the lawyers involved, rather than being used for cleaning up contaminated sites. The result is often bankruptcy for the small business owner, which helps no one.

Interestingly, small business and environmentalists are on the same side in this issue. Dragging small polluters (those who contribute less than 1 percent of hazardous waste at a particular site) into the litigation only slows the cleanup process without generating significant financial compensation. Environmentalists recognize that small polluters rarely can afford the costs of cleanup or penalties. That is why NFIB, in conjunction with the Environmental Defense Fund, the Sierra Club and the National Resources Defense Council, have been working together to find a pro-active solution.

In February 1994, NFIB lobbyist Harriet James outlined the coalition's recommendations in testimony before the House Subcommittee on Transportation and Hazardous Materials. By eliminating third-party litigation and replacing it with the proposed informal process, the EPA could streamline the allocation of responsibility among all parties involved in a Superfund site. The program calls for financial incentives to the EPA to allocate responsibility within 18 months, after which a small business would be released from liability if the EPA failed to make a settlement offer.

An important provision requires the EPA to take into account a small business' ability to pay. Businesses having fewer than 20 employees and less than $1.8 million in annual sales would receive special consideration and be presumed unable to pay – and relieved of liability – unless proven otherwise. NFIB also recommended that the EPA be required to develop an installment plan to allow small businesses to pay any penalties over time. In addition, a small businesses assistance office would be established.

Due to strong support among small business and environmental groups, it is almost certain these recommendations will be part of the Superfund reform bill. The legislation was in the early stages at presstime, but action on the floor is expected before the end of the 103rd Congress.

Clean Water Act

Another 1994 priority for Congress is the reauthorization of the Federal Water Pollution Control Act (commonly known as the Clean Water Act), the principal law governing pollution in the nation's streams, lakes and estuaries. A comprehensive Clean Water Act reauthorization bill, S. 1114, was introduced by Senators Max Baucus, D-Mont., and John H. Chafee, R-R.I., in June 1993, and both houses seem to be aiming towards final passage prior to the 1994 elections.

The Clean Water Act is probably the most successful of the federal environmental programs that currently exist. The statute has achieved tremendous improvements in water quality, most notably since passage of amendments in 1987 that created substantial new programs to address water quality concerns, particularly for toxic pollutants.

While reauthorizing the effective portions of the Clean Water Act, the Baucus-Chafee bill unfortunately also would add unnecessarily aggressive "command and control" features and uncalled-for enforcement mechanisms that would serve to expand the authority of the EPA, while offering no true improvements. These new features would only increase the compliance and paperwork burden on businesses, not make our water cleaner.

This broadened enforcement authority will open the door to increased litigation against small businesses – with little environmental benefit. Under the bill, courts can order violators of the Clean Water Act to restore "damaged natural resources" to their original condition. However, the provision provides no criteria to assess the extent of damage caused, no identification or limitation of the circumstances in which a court may order restoration, no basis for allocating costs, and virtually no cost control parameters. Like Superfund, this legislation has the potential to bankrupt companies deemed liable by the EPA, profiting only the attorneys involved.

Civil penalties can go as high as $5,000 per day for each violation, to a total of $25,000. Additionally, the EPA administrator has the authority to assess fines of up to $25,000 per day for violators found to have released "threatening" discharges. The only recourse for these companies is to pay the assessment or request a hearing of the charges, risking higher fines. The potential for abuse – using the program as a tool to fill EPA coffers – is obvious.

Many of these so-called "violators" are small companies that are genuinely trying to be in compliance. They simply do not have the financial capability to hire the lawyers necessary to interpret the regulations. That is why NFIB is pursuing the incorporation of a small business technical assistance program. Specifically, the program would include a voluntary audit program to help small businesses achieve full compliance. Small business owners want clean water as much as everyone else, and most act in good faith to be in compliance with the law. The goal of the EPA should be to help companies comply for the overall benefit of the environment. Making the regulations virtually impossible to understand while imposing harsher penalties for non-compliance is no answer.

Private Property Rights

Carol and Ed Wetmiller have owned and operated the Wapakoneta KOA campground and mobile home park since 1970. In all that time the facility's needs have been adequately served by one well, capped by a small pump that handles about 10 gallons a minute. But the Wetmillers realized it would be a good idea to have a backup well in case they ever had mechanical problems with the pump. So they called the Environmental Protection Agency in 1992 for advice on the proper procedures for drilling a new well.

"Besides telling us where we had to drill and how much it would cost to test the well (about $1,000), they calculated how much water this new well would have to produce per minute to meet their requirements. It was that last part that did us in," Carol Wetmiller said.

Rather than basing its calculations on occupation rate at the campground, the EPA figured how much water would be needed for all camping sites, mobile home sites, washing machines and showers at once. They came up with 80 gallons a minute, an amount that would require a huge, expensive pump.

The Wetmillers had to install a water meter to prove (after five months) that their highest water needs peaked at 7,200 gallons in one 24-hour period, an average of 5 gallons a minute. Yet, according to the weird math employed by the EPA, they were told they still needed 68 gallons per minute.

In frustration, they closed their mobile home park to lower the requirements and get new calculations. The EPA came back with 48 gallons a minute. "We couldn't understand how they kept getting these outrageous numbers and we pressed," she recalled.

The answer: after figuring the amount needed on the tables, the EPA then multiplied the answer by 10. The EPA's original calculation was, in fact, 8 gallons a minute, arbitrarily increased to 80. Incredibly, the EPA had no reason for the multiplication factor. They just did it. "We pressed and discovered they have no scientific study to support it," she said. Their bottom line? "We closed our mobile home park permanently and have not added a new well."

Our bottom line? Americans' basic Constitutional property rights are being held hostage by an unelected bureaucracy of federal agencies that wield uncontrollable power and use it to bully and extort law-abiding citizens for profit. This abuse is particularly common in the areas of wetlands preservation and the enforcement of the Endangered Species Act and the Resource Conservation and Recovery Act.

Wetlands

Yes, the Constitution does provide for the government – for specific reasons – to take private land for its own use, but not without compensating the owners. Lawful examples include building new highways or damming rivers. An example that small business owners contend is unlawful – because compensation is not provided – is the seizure of property that has been declared a wetland.

This problem intensified in 1989 when the U.S. Fish and Wildlife Service and the Army Corps of Engineers began using a new delineation manual that broadened the definition of a wetland. Under that definition, property as small as a ditch that sometimes contains water can technically be classified a wetland. This, in essence, prevents farmers and business owners from using their own land, yet does not compensate them for the lost use and value. Under this system, their Constitutional rights are being denied by an unelected bureaucracy of federal agencies.

Legislation to right this wrong was introduced during the 102nd Congress, which failed to act upon it. The Comprehensive Wetlands Conservation and Management Act recognized that all wetlands are not created equal. Some, such as swamps and marshes that sustain a variety of wildlife and keep an ecosystem in balance, are more important than others. The bill classified wetlands into three categories, keeping the top third – "most environmentally valuable" – areas under strict regulation and easing restrictions on others. The bill also established parameters for compensation.

It is hoped that some kind of wetlands reform bill that takes into consideration the property rights of individuals and businesses will be reintroduced, if not in 1994, then in 1995. Environmentalists should welcome this reform, as it will allow regulatory agencies to focus on the most important wetland areas. It may also deflect part of the criticism aimed at environmental issues as a whole from those who have been needlessly hurt by the mismanaged system.

Endangered Species

The same wish goes for the Endangered Species Act (ESA): It shouldn't have to be a point of contention between environmentalists and small business. No one advocates the wanton destruction of an entire species, and at the same time, no one wants to see double-digit unemployment wrecking the economy of an entire region.

Many who have studied the problem conclude that the ESA is a misdirected and mismanaged law. It is a law of absolutes that ignores its own impact and offers no means of redress. This is because the law is not flexible enough to be adapted to the individual environmental situations it was intended to address. Specific amendments are needed to bring the ESA under control.

The initial problem with the ESA is the unrealistic task that Congress set for it. More than 1,200 species and sub-species were originally listed as endangered or threatened, 676 of them in the United States. Another 3,500 more are waiting to be added, and the Natural Heritage data base has reported as many as 9,000 domestic species at risk.

Another difficulty with the law is the scope in which it acts. Stopping a proposed shopping center is one thing.

Disrupting the economies of multi-state regions is another. This is because the ESA lists certain species that are neither few in number nor confined to a few small sites. Some species, among them the Northern Spotted Owl, Snake River Sockeye Salmon and Desert Tortoise have large populations across several states.

Yet for them, landowners are prohibited from reasonable (and rightful) uses of their property, such as clearing brush, building homes or grazing livestock. Land values have been depressed or destroyed in cavalier disregard of the Constitutional protection of property rights. Although amendments to provide processes for landowners seeking relief were added to the ESA in 1978 and 1982, the unrealistic costs, long delays and insurmountable procedural barriers have allowed little actual relief.

The Resource Conservation and Recovery Act

Environmental laws are often too technical for the average American to understand, much less comply with. Small business owners care about cleaning up the environment. Unlike many officers of large corporations, they usually live in the same community where their businesses operate. But they cannot afford the lawyers, permit specialists and staff engineers necessary to decipher the regulations with which they must comply. So they end up doing the best they can and hoping they won't get burned.

This is especially true with the Resource Conservation

and Recovery Act (RCRA), the nation's primary solid and hazardous waste law. RCRA is due to be reauthorized, possibly this year, and small business owners should be alert for any changes that would increase their regulatory burden.

Yet, sometimes, even avoiding one burden only leads to others. For example, Fred Matricardi, president of A to Z Equipment Rentals & Sales in Phoenix, chose to get rid of the four underground fuel tanks on his property to avoid the expense of the EPA's new stringent requirements. He had used the tanks to fuel the gasoline- and diesel-powered equipment he rents, without having to drive to a gas station and fill up cans of fuel.

Of course, in several decades some spillage had occurred, meaning tons of dirt had to be removed. Matricardi estimated the total cost will top $40,000, including his initial investment, removing the tanks and dirt, filling in the holes and repaving. It does not include returning to his old system of sending trucks filled with gas cans to local fuel stations, which wastes labor and time. "And the net savings to the environment?" he asked. "Zero. There are going to be as many spills as there were before, maybe more."

Toxic spills are the subject of another RCRA provision that all small business owners should keep an eye on. It is the proposed Community Right to Know More legislation, which seeks to expand the Emergency Planning and Community Right to Know Act of 1986. The original act established annual toxic chemical reporting requirements for 320 substances. It applies to facilities in 19 SIC codes, mainly manufacturers, who employ 10 or more people. Coverage is restricted to facilities that generate 25,000 pounds per year or use 10,000 pounds per year of any one of the listed chemicals.

The new Right to Know More legislation seeks to expand reporting and handling requirements. It would:

•Significantly lower reporting thresholds.

•Expand reportable substances from 320 to 570.

•Expand coverage to 17 additional SIC codes with more to be included at regular intervals.

•Require "peak release reports," potentially requiring hourly monitoring of possible chemical releases.

Businesses covered by the legislation include bakeries, gas stations, dry cleaners, auto body repair shops, pharmacies and restaurants. It would increase the number of covered business from 29,000 to more than 100,000, increasing the government's administration costs, as well. Even if small businesses don't meet the lowered threshold of chemical releases, they would be required to monitor and evaluate chemical use to determine if they do meet it.

On the positive side, some amendments would change RCRA for the better. The previous RCRA draft included a provision directing the EPA to develop a technical assistance program to help small businesses meet environmental goals. The language, however, was vague. It provided no eligibility guidelines or indication of what elements of compliance should be covered. Small business owners need RCRA amendments specifying: technical assistance with compliance, access to "no fault" audits, enforcement flexibility, limits on continuous monitoring and representation by small business owners on state compliance advisory panels.

Whether RCRA, or any of the current environmental regulations, can be changed for the better is up to Congress. But their votes can be swayed if enough people get involved. Small business owners must be active in government issues, because the government certainly is active in theirs. For information on what small business owners can do to communicate their views to the right people, see Chapter 8 and the following Small Business Survival Guide.

7

State Government: Proof That the Siege Can Be Broken

---

ynics – some might say realists – swear that being in government causes otherwise well-meaning people to lose touch with the real needs and concerns of constituents. Their well-intentioned efforts to address some perceived inequity or wrong often serve to reinforce those who actively disregard or discount small business' contribution to the economic life of this country.

Nevertheless, while small businesses rightly complain about the impact federal policies make on them, it is often state laws that have the most adverse effect on their day-to-day operations. Sometimes, even when one arm of government acts to help business owners, another arm puts them right back in a hammerlock.

Consider the case of Eileen Cummings, sole proprietor of Inky Dew, a La Mesa, Calif., company that recycles computer printer ribbons, who describes pointedly how government's lack of flexibility hurts businesses.

"The recent Workers' Compensation Law (reform) ... was supposed to decrease my rates by 7 percent," she said, noting she did get a refund and a reduced premium – at first. "One week later, my premium was increased because my audit changed my classification. They don't know where to classify my business because it's obviously never been done before to their knowledge."

This was in August 1993. She requested an on-site audit in November and in February was still waiting for a ruling on her classification. Meanwhile, she has to pay the higher rates and what is worse, "I've had to cut my employees' hours from 30-40 per week to 8-10 per week!"

Among the top issues that crop up repeatedly in state legislative sessions are workers' compensation, health care reform, litigation reform and taxation. NFIB and its members work hard to educate lawmakers about the concerns of small business owners. Increasingly, small business owners have become more involved in the political process themselves as another means of bringing about change in the system.

And, although it may seem that the onslaught never stops, the good news is that small business owners have in recent years had some success in stopping or at least blunting many of the most onerous anti-business initiatives. Most of this book has dealt with how government encroachment holds small business under siege. In the chapter on health care, you saw how the strong, consistent reaction of small business appears to be deflecting employer-mandated health care coverage. In the chapter on the environment, you learned how small business has influenced revisions in Superfund legislation. These achievements are mirrored on the state level. The following pages offer a message of hope, for they show how small business owners and the NFIB together can make a difference when state governments try to intervene in business.

Workers' Compensation

Fraud, abuse, exorbitant premiums, increased downtime, higher health care costs, lost jobs – the list of complaints against states' workers' compensation systems seems endless. And equally, it seems that for organized labor and trial lawyers, a legislative session without a bill to increase WC benefits is like a day without sunshine.

But lately, the sun has been shining on small business' side of the street. In state after state, lawmakers have realized the negative effects of unchecked WC programs on the business climate. State governments have launched meaningful crackdowns on fraud, waste and abuse, which experts estimate comprise from 5 to 25 percent of the cost of workers' compensation. They have turned back efforts to needlessly expand benefits at the expense of business.

For example:

•**Connecticut**'s far-reaching workers' compensation reform bill adopted in the 1993 legislative session is considered a landmark piece of legislation. NFIB played a leadership role in passage of this sweeping reform package constructed by a bipartisan coalition and advocated by the administration. The reform contains a 20 percent reduction in costs of the Connecticut workers' compensation system. This means up to a 20 percent premium savings for businesses. This legislation is also the most far-reaching economic development and jobs incentive package ever passed in Connecticut, worth more than $200 million.

In addition, through the Nutmeg State's Workers' Compensation Fraud Statute, the legislature created a separate prosecutor in the Division of Criminal Justice to prosecute WC fraud. The Workers' Compensation Fraud Unit prosecutes all crimes relating to the fraudulent receipt or payment of workers' compensation benefits, and is funded through administrative assessment on premiums. WC fraud also was made a criminal offense.

•On Dec. 1, 1993, **Florida's** governor signed into law a workers' compensation reform package that is expected to reduce premium rates more than 25 percent. A large portion of the savings, approximately 17 percent, are "do-it-yourself" initiatives – businesses that opt for a managed care policy, establish a drug-free workplace and a safety program, and participate in the deductible program are eligible to receive the full savings. The legislature did not set a rate reduction into law as they did in 1990 due to actuarial uncertainty concerning the total savings in the package. But NFIB expects the insurance commissioner will issue a rate decrease of 10 to 11 percent. Businesses that take advantage of the optional initiatives could realize even greater savings.

•In a move predicted to save **California** employers as much as $1 billion, the insurance commission slashed workers' comp premiums by 12.7 percent. This is the biggest reduction of its kind ever in California. These cuts are the direct result of reforms that NFIB supported the previous year.

•In **New York**, a workers' comp reform act will provide immediate rate relief and lay the groundwork for the long-term stability of rates through managed care. In early 1993, more than 450 business owners lobbied legislators to urge passage of a managed care bill. The bill passed the Senate unanimously, and cleared the Assembly with only one "no" vote.

Litigation

One classic definition of inflation is too much money chasing too few goods. Thus, one wonders if the abundance of lawyers in our society contributes to the ever-increasing number of lawsuits, many of which have little or no merit. Whatever the cause, our overly litigious society has helped push liability insurance premiums sky-high for small business owners.

The tort liability system in the United States is by far the most expensive in the industrialized world. U.S. tort costs are 2.3 percent of Gross Domestic Product. The direct cost of the litigation is $132 billion annually, yet less than 50 cents of each dollar awarded is actually paid to victims.

Legislation is pending before Congress that would provide some reforms to product liability laws. Instead of a hodgepodge of state laws, there would be one national liability system with a uniform standard for punitive damages. There would also be incentives to settle out of court and a time limit to protect businesses from suits against products more than 25 years old. The legislation also would eliminate joint and several liability for non-economic damages like pain and suffering. Businesses would be liable only in proportion to their share of responsibility, instead of full damages. These changes, besides easing the insurance burden on businesses, would also lead ultimately to lower prices for consumers.

Nationwide, state legislatures have begun to recognize the plight of small companies and are coming to their aid.

•In Juneau, the **Alaska** legislature is considering comprehensive tort reform that would amend the Alaska Civil Liability Act by clarifying language and establishing time limits and award guidelines. The reform act is intended to permit fair compensation to prevailing parties, prevent inflated judgments, and allow fair payment to attorneys. Meanwhile, the legislature has approved a law providing protection for employers from civil law suits for disclosing job information on employees.

•In **Colorado**, 89.5 percent of NFIB members support a proposal to require the losing party in a civil suit to reimburse the costs, including legal fees, of the prevailing party. If a party prevails in some respects and loses in others, costs are apportioned. If a plaintiff recovers less than

132

the amount claimed, it is regarded as a partial defeat and cost recovery is reduced accordingly. The goal of this legislation is to reduce frivolous litigation while protecting the rights of individuals to seek redress.

•A similar goal has been set in **Illinois**, where an NFIB-led coalition hopes to curb "junk" lawsuits. The 100-member Illinois Civil Justice League includes the Illinois Medical Society, Illinois Business Round Table, Illinois Petroleum Council and the Regional Transportation Authority. The group has targeted non-economic damages (such as emotional distress damages), punitive damages, frivolous litigation and product liability. Also, Illinois' governor and the leader of the state Senate have made tort reform a priority.

•Sometimes reform comes in an unusual guise. In **Ohio** just over a year ago, the jurisdiction of small claims court was doubled, from $1,000 to $2,000. A bill has been introduced to raise it to $10,000. This is good news for small businesses, since small claims court can provide swift, hassle-free resolution of business problems such as bad check collection, theft, unfulfilled contracts and customer dissatisfaction. But court costs can exceed jurisdictional limits, meaning plaintiffs could end up paying more in court costs than the amount of the judgment they are seeking. By raising jurisdictional limits, small businesses can pursue claims with the hope of collecting meaningful judgments.

Health Care

Small businesses owners worried about health care insurance long before the present national debate began (see Chapter 3). They were worried about the cost of buying insurance, the rising cost of keeping it, and, too often, the inability to get it at any price.

State governments have also worried about health care for some years, as the cost of federal-state programs such as Medicaid soared beyond the ability of taxpayers to support them. Rather than wait for Washington, many states have either already implemented changes in health care policy or are actively considering them. A number of the proposed solutions are founded on employer mandates, the foundation of the administration's Health Security Act. But, thanks to quick action by NFIB members, alternatives to these proposals have been put forth to eliminate or ameliorate employer mandates in several states. These alternatives have also addressed some of small business' primary concerns about the health insurance industry.

•In 1992 in **California**, for instance, NFIB sponsored legislation to change the way that health insurance was offered in the small business market. The laws, which took effect in 1993, prohibit preexisting condition requirements and prohibit "cherry picking" (insuring low- risk groups) by insurance companies. In addition, the legislature created the Health Insurance Plan of California (HIPC) to provide an alternative means of offering health care coverage to small businesses who could not otherwise afford coverage.

In 1994, the Golden State's legislature will consider several comprehensive health care reform plans. NFIB will oppose any plan which seeks to require small business owners to pay for health coverage. The possible plans are as follows:

1. "Play or Pay" approach – Employers would be required to pay a penalty assessment to the state if they did not pay for health insurance coverage. The penalty would be equal to the cost of a premium.

2. Universal Single Payer System – Employers would be required to pay for health insurance coverage through a 13 percent payroll tax. The state would provide health insurance coverage to all Californians, as well as paying doctors' salaries and hospital bills. Insurance companies would, in effect, cease to write health coverage policies there.

3. Mandated Regional Purchasing Agencies – Employers would be mandated to pay for health insurance for their employees through an as yet unspecified payroll tax. Health coverage would be provided through a number of regional agencies that would contract with local providers for the cost of care.

•After **Coloradans** spoke out at a series of public forums, the governor has dropped plans for ColoradoCare, a universal health care plan based on an employer-mandated payroll tax – at least temporarily. Citizens objected strenuously to more taxes, even to obtain universal coverage. However, the governor has said he may put ColoradoCare back on the table once Washington has decided the issue at the federal level and if the state has not acted to remedy the problem. NFIB and other members of the business community aren't waiting. They have formed the Employer Coalition for Health Care Reform, which, with assistance from NFIB staff, will present several proposals that emphasize the free market solutions rather than government involvement. The Coalition's three proposals dramatically change the insurance marketplace and contain costs.

One bill would create voluntary cooperative purchasing pools that would enable small employers to purchase group insurance at lower rates.

A second bill would change the way insurance companies do business in Colorado by expanding NFIB-supported reforms enacted in 1991 and 1992. The small group health insurance reform bill would require insurance companies to offer basic, affordably priced insurance to any employer with fewer than 50 employees, with no pre-existing condition exclusions. Self-employed individuals will also be able to purchase basic insurance because they will be considered groups of one. If successful, the Colorado business community will have pushed insurance companies further than any other state toward universal access and modified community rating.

A third bill offers cost containment legislation. Building on the recommendations of the Guaranteed Access and Cost Containment Commission in which NFIB participated, the bill focuses on increasing the supply of primary care providers, publishing accurate and understandable information on hospitals and on outpatient outcomes, promoting healthy lifestyles in the basic benefit plan, and eliminating excess capacity through tax policy incentives.

•**Maryland** last year passed a health care bill that makes a standard, affordable health plan available to small businesses on a voluntary basis. Coverage cannot be refused on the grounds of prior health history of employees and risk will be spread across the entire small business market, not shouldered by a single small company.

•**Wisconsin** legislators recently concluded debate on the governor's Health Care Partnership Plan, which would allow for voluntary employer/employee participation in large purchasing pools to give small businesses sufficient purchasing power and negotiating leverage to reduce their health care costs. Competing for lawmakers' attention was a single-payer, publicly financed system that would have put state government in charge of health care. Funding would have come from a new tax on employers and higher taxes for all.

•**Tennessee** has presented small businesses with not one, but two paths of health care coverage reform.

Beginning Jan. 1, 1994, small employers – those with 3 to 25 employees – could purchase their choice of one of two new guaranteed-issue major medical plans: a standard plan or a lower-cost basic plan. In 1992, the Tennessee Legislature with the support of NFIB passed this act for the purpose of assuring the availability and access of health insurance to small employers. The act also provides greater renewability guarantees and sets time limits on preexisting condition exclusions. The primary drawback is that insurers will be able to price the policies to offset the guaranteed-issue risks.

Also beginning Jan. 1, 1994, the state replaced its Medicaid system with a program called TennCare, which also will offer coverage to many uninsured and underinsured working citizens. Employees who were uninsured as of March 1, 1993, and continued to be uninsured as of January 1994, could apply for TennCare. The program offers a benefit package comparable to that enjoyed by state employees. The lowest-income workers may not be required to pay deductibles or copayments, while those with higher wages will pay some level of deductibles, copayments and premiums.

Taxation

Every level of government imposes taxes. As federal outlays to the states continue to diminish, levies by states, counties, cities, school districts and numerous other bodies increase.

Sometimes a tax wears a disguise, as when it is called a mandatory health insurance premium or a fee, for example. Whatever they are called, taxes will always be with us. Small businesses must be on guard against unfair or punitive levies, and work to inform legislators that excessive taxation in the long run tends to reduce actual revenues.

•With passage of the "It's TIME!" initiative in **Arizona**, which requires a two-thirds majority in the legislature to raise taxes or fees, lawmakers aren't even considering tax increases. But county and city governments are. To make sure the people have a say, NFIB members voted overwhelmingly (81 percent) in favor of requiring a two-thirds popular vote for tax or bond increases. A petition drive was being organized at presstime to try to put this proposal to the voters in the November 1994 general elections.

•NFIB has been joined by many other groups in **Iowa** in its drive to secure passage of a "Taxpayer Bill of Rights" later this year. The bill requires the Iowa Department of Revenue and Finance to furnish a written statement of rights for taxpayers whenever they receive an assessment, a bill, or a claim denial. It also improves rules on interest payments, burden-of-proof installment payments and notice of actions.

•Unemployment taxes make up an important component of businesses' annual tax bill. In **Massachusetts**, the governor in late 1993 signed into law an act that prevents an automatic 22 percent rate increase in 1994 unemployment insurance taxes. The legislation will save employers $180 million in 1994. NFIB members pushed their legislators hard to support this issue, and were rewarded by unanimous support in the House and Senate. Since 1985, the unemployment insurance tax had increased an average of 117 percent, as compared with the Consumer Price Index which increased 28 percent during the same time. Massachusetts' unemployment insurance trust fund had been bled dry because of the state's large number of unemployed and its high benefit levels. The Commonwealth had been forced to borrow from the federal government to pay benefits since 1991. However, recent projections by the Department of Employment and Training indicate that the trust fund will be solvent by the end of 1994, thus eliminating the need for the increase.

8

Help Lift the Siege on Small Business – What You Can Do

———

T hroughout the course of this book, you have read how vital the health of small business is to the economy of our country. You've also read how small business' health is declining due to increasing regulatory burdens, burying America's job-creating engine under a mountain of time-consuming paperwork, costly mandates and incomprehensible rules. After learning all this, the time has come to ask: Are you going to sit there and take it? Or are you going to do something about it?

Are you going "to suffer the slings and arrows of outrageous fortune, or to take arms against a sea of troubles, and by opposing end them?" as William Shakespeare more eloquently asked.

"Put up or shut up" is a good modern interpretation. Whatever. You get the point.

Maybe, though, you doubt that you could make much difference in such a contest That might be true, if you were fighting this battle alone. But you don't have to try to go it alone.

As a member of the National Federation of Independent Business, the oldest, largest and most effective small business advocacy organization in the country, you become part of an army 600,000 strong. With these voices in unison, NFIB delivers a rousing chorus that those on Capitol Hill and in the White House, as well as legislatures in all 50 states, must listen to.

Founded in 1943, NFIB has for more than half a century devoted itself to protecting the free-enterprise system. In a recent *Wall Street Journal* article, one Washington, D.C., lobbyist compares NFIB's approach to those of other lobbying groups. Some, he said, make their reputation because they know certain senators or committee chairmen personally. NFIB, however, gets its strength "from being able to get tens of thousands of people across the country to do something."

Why is that? Because, said John Motley, NFIB's vice president of federal government relations, "Before we act, we ask." NFIB is the voice of small businesses in America, which, unlike large corporations, cannot afford spokespersons to explain their points of view to the nation's leaders. As their voice, NFIB does not take its responsibility lightly. NFIB determines its position on key issues solely through bimonthly surveys of its membership and acts only when a clear mandate is provided. NFIB sends the results of each poll, business by business, to all 535 congressional offices. So, in effect, NFIB members have the opportunity to voice their opinions in Washington every two months, rather than every four years.

Besides participating in these surveys, there are other steps that you can take to get your concerns heard by state and federal lawmakers. If you are already a member of NFIB and are concerned about government's effect on your business, consider getting more involved as suggested below. If you are not an NFIB member, but are concerned, there is always room in the army for more soldiers willing to fight for free enterprise. The following will show how you can help.

Make Friends in High Places

Naturally, having a personal relationship with an elected official is the best way to convey your interests. If you are already acquainted with your state or federal legislators, you have a distinct opportunity that you should exploit. Lawmakers are not mind readers. They depend on their constituents to tell them what issues are important back home – and they value voters who can back up their opinions with concrete facts and real-world experiences. As an employer in your legislator's hometown or home state, you are just such a person.

Your opinions count. But you might not know how to let your elected officials know what your interests are. Or you may not have all the information you need to decide on a position. Let NFIB help. Through NFIB's "Key Contact" program, you can become part of an extensive grass-roots network of small business owners like yourself, who have the advantage of a personal acquaintance with their state or federal legislators.

If you are not acquainted with any of your elected officials, there is no time like the present to introduce yourself. The best place to do that is right where you are, in the legislator's home district where the votes are cast. Getting to know your elected officials at home may help you obtain better access to them when they return to their sessions at the state capital or in Washington and are voting on an issue important to you.

How do you meet your elected official? It's not hard. In fact, it may be as easy as calling the official's office, asking when he or she will be in the area, and requesting an appointment. On the phone or in a letter, explain that you are a business owner within the legislator's district and that you wish to discuss your positions on certain issues or legislation that you expect to be addressed by the legislative body.

Remember, your insights are important. As an employer in the legislator's district, your business has a direct impact on the economic health of the community. And the best way to communicate your perspective is in person. You may wish to bring a fellow small business owner or two to the meeting to add the power of numbers to your position, but don't overdo it. You don't want to create a confrontational atmosphere. You want to establish a rapport with your legislator to keep the door open for future contact. Making him or her uncomfortable on the first visit wouldn't help.

When you call for an appointment, make clear who you are and what you have to offer. Obviously, just being a constituent makes you important, but other information might help you stand out from the rest. It may be a certain piece of legislation will impact your business directly. Then say so: "I've just started a plumbing supply business that employs nine people, and I'd like to discuss with the congresswoman how her vote on health care reform will affect my ability to stay in business and possibly increase employment in this community."

Your previous support is also worth noting: "I contributed to the senator's campaign because I knew he understood the problems facing small business owners in this area. Now that worker's compensation is on the agenda, I wanted to let him know how his vote will affect my grocery store and the 17 employees who depend on me."

Even if all you did was vote for the legislator, say so. And if you didn't, that's OK. Most lawmakers welcome the chance to meet with doubters in order to turn them into future supporters. Tell them that's exactly what you intend to be – if they show you a firm commitment to promoting small business issues.

Be specific about the issues that concern you most. Limit yourself to one or two topics. You can't hit them all at once, so stick to the ones on which you can best comment: topics that have affected or will affect you directly. Once you've established a relationship, you'll have opportunities to offer opinions on other subjects.

Climbing the Ladder

Don't get discouraged if you don't get an appointment on your first try. Scheduling a face-to-face meeting between two busy people is no simple task. If you are unable to meet with the legislator, ask to meet with the aide assigned to the specific issue that concerns you. Establishing an acquaintance with an aide may eventually lead to a direct meeting with the legislator.

Legislative staff members are important contacts to make. Lawmakers face so many issues of such a technical nature, there is no way one person could be an expert on all of them. So they rely heavily on their staffs, who research the issues and provide background information on which legislators can base their voting decisions. Your real-world experiences can be an important part of the research that influences their votes.

Presenting your point of view in a concise, reasoned manner will make an impression. It may open the opportunity for future contact on other business issues. And the staffer you help may be the person who can slice through the bureaucratic red tape later, when you need to communicate to your legislator your views on a critical issue.

A Public Forum

Sometimes, a one-on-one meeting, even with an aide, cannot be conveniently set up. There are plenty of other opportunities. When you call your legislator's office, ask when the legislator is planning a town meeting or other public forum, such as a speech to some civic group. These hometown meetings are important to lawmakers and their constituents as a way of keeping in touch with the public opinion.

Often, the legislator schedules public forums to drum up support for a particular piece of legislation. Whether you agree or disagree with the bill, attend the meeting and find a way to relate the subject to your situation. For example, you might say, "I would happily support this health care reform bill, if it offered an incentive to employers for providing health insurance, rather than mandating coverage. As it exists now, I would have to lay off half a dozen people to pay for it."

Don't be hostile, even if the legislator disagrees with you. Maintaining a professional dialog is the key. Maybe on another issue down the road, your professionalism will convince the legislator to vote your way.

Even if the forum subject has little to do with you, you can attend for the sole reason of meeting your elected official. Arrive early and stay late to increase your opportunities. Be honest about why you're there. "This new highway bill doesn't directly affect me, but I came anyway to hear your point of view. I hoped to meet you and introduce myself because some of the bills you'll be voting on later will directly affect me and my printing business."

Don't try to buttonhole the legislator for an hour. He or she will be too busy meeting other constituents at the forum. After you introduce yourself, state your concern and request a private meeting with the legislator or an aide to discuss it.

Face-to-Face

When you do get an appointment with your legislator or staff aide, arrive prepared. This person's time is as valuable as yours, so don't overstay your welcome. Be pleasant, but get right to the issue you came to discuss. Begin with a commendation, if that is appropriate, thanking the legislator for past support of small business issues.

Present your case in a businesslike manner, using concrete examples from your experience: "My margins are as low as a business can have and stay afloat. The last time the minimum wage was increased, I had to lay off two people, which increased the work load on the remaining employees. Production went down. It took us more than a year to recover, and I still haven't been able to grow and add new employees."

If you need background information on any state or federal issue, NFIB can help. On state issues, call your NFIB state director. (Check the NFIB state phone directory in the following Survival Guide chapter.) For federal issues, you can call NFIB's Washington, D.C., legislative staff at (202) 554-9000.

If it becomes apparent that you aren't going to sway the legislator to vote the way you want, keep the conversation good-natured. People are more receptive to calm, intelligent reasoning than to harsh criticism. Even if you are not successful, your professionalism will be remembered. You may later get the opportunity to discuss other key issues – and win.

Receptive Ears

Just think how great it will feel to find your representative responsive to the small business position. Respond in kind. Let him or her know you plan to continue your political support and volunteer your time.

First, ask to become a member of the legislator's business advisory board, so you can help her or him keep informed of how hometown voters view pending legislation that affects small businesses and the community.

Keep up with how your elected officials vote on small business issues. And when re-election bids start up, volunteer to assist the campaigns of those who have demonstrated support for your interests.

Take Pen in Hand

While you are waiting for the opportunity to meet with your legislator or an aide, use that time to contact your legislator by letter. Written contact is generally less effective than a personal meeting, but it may lead to one. In addition, it is the best way to register your point of view on specific matters when time is short, such as when important legislation comes up for a vote.

As in a face-to-face meeting, introduce yourself and explain why your opinion counts: your business, how many you employ, how you are directly affected by the particular issue. As stated above, limit yourself to one topic and keep your message concise and well-reasoned, using specific examples from your business experience. Be clear about what you want, as well. Tell your legislator to "vote yes" or "vote no," introduce a helpful amendment to a bill, etc.

Always conclude with a request to meet with the legislator or an aide to discuss the issue further. If you are unsure how to word your letter or desire additional background information on the subject, NFIB can help.

Don't feel slighted if your letter is answered with a standard form reply. Legislators receive a lot of mail and can't write a personal response to each letter. Any response puts the ball back in your court, so return it. Write an answer to the answer, beginning it with a thank-you to the legislator for the response.

If the reply indicates that your elected official has not yet decided how to vote on the issue you've raised, provide another example or two of how you will be affected by the vote. Mention other examples from your business associates who might also be affected. If the legislator's reply mentioned counter-reasons, address them thoughtfully.

If the legislator's reply letter indicates how he or she will act, your response must either: commend the legislator for taking a pro-small business stance and promise your support; or express regret that the legislator does not recognize how detrimental this action will be to the livelihood of small business constituents back home. Whichever response is appropriate, keep the door open for future contact.

Press Pass

While a personal discourse is important, don't ignore the power of the mass media. Raising or addressing an issue publicly gets the attention not only of your elected officials, but also of others in the community who can add their voices to yours. Legislators use their hometown media to stay in touch with events and issues in their districts. A letter to the editor of your local newspaper or television station can get the ball rolling to an open dialogue on important issues.

Your letters should be brief, using specific examples of how you are or will be directly affected by the issue at hand. Use a reasoned, non-combative tone, but don't be surprised if your letter draws a negative response. To those who disagree with you, immediately counter their arguments in a professional, non-hostile manner. This serves to keep the issue alive and better catch the attention of readers or viewers, including your legislative audience.

You may also get the attention of reporters. News

reporters are always looking for a local angle on a national story. You may end up being quoted in a news story. Remember that reporters must often report on topics they themselves do not fully understand, frequently under tight deadlines. They may ask background questions that seem obvious to you. Or they may want a comment from you with very short notice.

If you are asked to be interviewed on camera, don't be shy. Review what you want to say and say it as briefly as possible. Sometimes a concrete example is all that's needed: "If this shoplifting legislation passes, I could prevent $5,000 a year in losses. That's money I could use to expand my business."

Your willingness to help reporters complete their stories thoroughly and accurately may open doors for future media access. Reporters value a good source. The next time a small business issue comes up, your opinion may be solicited again. Take advantage of every opportunity.

Word of Mouth

Participating in community service groups, religious organizations, special interest clubs and student associations is another way to promote the interests of small business. From informal conversations to classroom discussions to public speaking, "word of mouth" travels far.

School affiliations are of particular importance. Speaking to a government class or civics club is an excellent way to shape young minds. And, who knows? One of those kids might one day grow up to be a legislator or president, or even better – a fellow small business owner. They may one day credit you for sparking their interest.

Of course, public speaking is not for everybody. But with practice, a person can learn to channel natural nervous energy into contagious enthusiasm. To learn how, contact your local community college. Most offer courses in public speaking. If your speech is to be covered by the media (even the school paper), distribute typed double-spaced copies of your talk beforehand, to ensure they quote you accurately.

Jump Into the Fray

Maybe your discussions with elected officials lead you to believe that no one is representing your interests in the legislature. If they won't, who will? Why not you? If you're tired of having government tell you how to run your business, turn the tables. More and more small business owners are using their valuable time to serve as state and federal legislators, changing the system from the inside.

You can help make your state and the nation a better place to do business. If your path leads that way, NFIB can help. Contact your state director for advice and assistance.

Get Involved in Any Way

No matter how you choose to be involved, the important thing is that you stay involved. You can – and will – make a difference. It's not just a right, it's an obligation. Communicating your views to your government leaders is the only way they will know how their vote affects their constituents. They can't ignore a chorus of more than 600,000 voices. And you are an important voice in that chorus, no matter which part you sing. Whether you run for office or just maintain your NFIB membership, your participation in the system ensures the continuance of small business' big voice in Washington, D.C.

NFIB's "Health Care and Grass Roots Activism" video and manual can help train you to communicate your concerns more effectively. The video details specifics of various health care plans, showing how each could affect your business. It also demonstrates techniques and principles that can help you become a more effective and active participant in the political process. The video is available for $19.95 and can be ordered by calling 1-800-NFIB-NOW.

9

Small Business Survival Guide

I t takes idealism, courage, tenacity and an entrepreneurial spirit to own or run a small business. Small business owners dream of watching their hard work flourish and turn into something more profitable and more successful than it was when they began. Small business ownership is about building dreams as much as it is about creating jobs.

In this chapter, you will find the names, the organizations and some of the words you'll need to help you continue to survive and succeed in the coming years, despite government's efforts to intrude on the operation of your business.

The outlook for many issues important to small business remains bright. There are still issues, however, around which small business advocates will need to join together to make their voices heard and their opinions known. It is only through this common effort and a carefully orchestrated strategy that small business interests will be taken seriously.

The previous chapter outlined how small business owners can get involved in lobbying for their cause. This chapter is devoted to the specifics of such efforts. Please use it as a handbook for making your opinions known and for ensuring that future generations have the same chance at individual success that you have had.

The National Federation of Independent Business

More than 99 percent of all businesses in America are small and independent businesses. The participation of every individual business owner is vital to influencing the political machine that affects all small business in America. But when individuals stand together, they carry more political weight, so Big Government will better hear you — and Big Business and Big Labor will think twice before they try to push you around.

The National Federation of Independent Business (NFIB) is a unified, powerful voice for all business owners like you. Because it is the largest, oldest and most effective organization of its kind, it has the collective clout of more than 600,000 members on its side to challenge state and federal legislation detrimental to your business.

NFIB is the nation's largest lobbying staff of its kind, with more than 75 state and federal lobbyists, and offices in every state capital and Washington, D.C. Perhaps most importantly, all stances NFIB takes on legislative issues are determined by member response to surveys. Membership in NFIB allows you to present the views of small and independent business before state and federal legislators with powerful facts, relevant research and the authority and collective clout of the members' votes on the issues. If you are not a member, see the membership enrollment form on the last page of this book to join, or contact one of the offices listed below. You may also call 1-800-274-NFIB (6342) for more information.

NFIB State Directors' Offices

Alabama
400 S. Union Street, Suite 465
Montgomery, AL 36104
Tel: 205-264-2261
Fax: 205-264-4252

Alaska
9159 Skywood Lane
Juneau, AK 99801
Tel: 907-789-4278
Fax: 907-789-3433

Arizona
101 W. Almeria
Phoenix, AZ 85003
Tel: 602-254-1541
Fax: 602-254-0354

Arkansas
221 West Second, Suite 621
Little Rock, AR 72201
Tel: 501-372-7593
Fax: 501-375-6001

California
980 9th Street, 16th Floor
Sacramento, CA 95814-2736
Tel: 916-448-9904
Fax: 916-448-5442

Colorado
1410 Grant Street, B104
Denver, CO 80203
Tel: 303-860-1778
Fax: 303-860-1787

Connecticut
88 Palmer Drive
South Windsor, CT 06074
Tel: 203-648-9201
Fax: 203-644-9950 (Call first)

Delaware
P.O. Box 504
Dover, DE 19901
Tel: 302-734-2275
Fax: 302-734-5164

Florida
One Capital Place
110 East Jefferson Street
Tallahassee, FL 32301
Tel: 904-681-0416
Fax: 904-561-6759

Georgia
1447 Peachtree St. N.E.
#1008
Atlanta, GA 30309
Tel: 404-876-8516
Fax: 404-876-1253

Hawaii
1588 Piikea
Honolulu, HI 96818
Tel: 808-422-2163
Fax: 808-422-2163

Idaho
277 N. 6th Street, Suite 200
Boise, ID 83702
Tel: 208-343-3289
Fax: 208-343-1368

Illinois
217 East Monroe Street
Suite 98A
Springfield, IL 62701
Tel: 217-523-5471
Fax: 217-523-3850

Indiana
101 West Ohio Street
Suite 570
Indianapolis, IN 46204
Tel: 317-638-4447
Fax: 317-638-4450

Iowa
319 E. 5th Street
Des Moines, IA 50309
Tel: 515-243-4723
Fax: 515-244-8143

Kansas
10039 Mastin Drive
Shawnee Mission, KS 66212
Tel: 913-888-2235
Fax: 913-273-9200

Kentucky
1501 Twilight Trail
Frankfort, KY 40601
Tel: 502-223-5322
Fax: 502-223-5322 (Call First)

Louisiana
8738 Quarters Lake Road
Suite 5
Baton Rouge, LA 70809
Tel: 504-922-9165
Fax: 504-922-9125

Maine
P.O. Box 4629
Portland, ME 04112-4629
Tel: 207-773-3326
Fax: 207-871-7597

Maryland
7910 Woodmont Ave.
Suite 1204
Bethesda, MD 20814
Tel: 301-652-0721
Fax: 301-657-1973

Massachusetts
101 Tremont Street
Suite 1001
Boston, MA 02108
Tel: 617-482-1327
Fax: 617-482-5286

Michigan
114 So. Grand Ave., Suite B
Lansing, MI 48933
Tel: 517-485-3409
Fax: 517-485-2155

Minnesota
26 E. Exchange St., Suite 319
St. Paul, MN 55101
Tel: 612-293-1283
Fax: 612-293-0084

Mississippi
3000 N. State St.
Jackson, MS 39216
Tel: 601-982-3332
Fax: 601-362-2909 (Sir Speedy)

Missouri
P.O. Box 1543
Jefferson City, MO 65102
Tel: 314-634-7660
Fax: 314-636-9749

Montana
491 South Park Ave.
Helena, MT 59601
Tel: 406-443-3797
Fax: 406-442-2107

Nebraska
525 South 13th Street, Suite 3
Lincoln, NE 68508
Tel: 402-474-3570
Fax: 402-474-2946

Nevada
301 W. Washington Street
Suite 2
Carson City, NV 89703
Tel: 702-883-1312
Fax: 702-883-1312

New Hampshire
P.O. Box 218
Concord, NH 03301
Tel: 603-228-3477
Fax: 603-226-0979

New Jersey
156 W. State Street
Trenton, NJ 08608
Tel: 609-989-8777
Fax: 609-393-0781

New Mexico
P.O. Box B546
Santa Fe, NM 87505
Tel: 505-471-5455
Fax: 505-471-5455 (call first)

New York
134 State Street, Suite 400
Albany, NY 12207
Tel: 518-434-1262
Fax: 518-426-8799

North Carolina
P.O. Box 710
Raleigh, NC 27602
Tel: 919-755-1166
Fax: 919-839-1492

North Dakota
1910 N. 11th Street, Suite 10
Bismarck, ND 58501
Tel: 701-224-8333
Fax: 701-223-8746

Ohio
50 West Broad Street
Suite 1321
Columbus, OH 43215
Tel: 614-221-4107
Fax: 614-221-8677

Oklahoma
515 Central Park Drive
Suite 403
Oklahoma City, OK 73105
Tel: 405-521-8967
Fax: 405-528-1462

Oregon
1241 State Street, Suite 211
Salem, OR 97301
Tel: 503-364-4450
Fax: 503-363-5814

Pennsylvania
City Towers, #809
301 Chestnut Street
Harrisburg, PA 17101
Tel: 717-232-8582
Fax: 717-232-4098

Rhode Island
159 Elmgrove Avenue
Providence, RI 02906
Tel: 401-421-8676
Fax: 401-421-3924

South Carolina
P.O. Box 244
Lexington, SC 29072
Tel: 803-359-6300
Fax: 803-359-3265

South Dakota
319 Coteau Street, Box 280
Pierre, SD 57501
Tel: 605-224-7102
Fax: 605-224-7102 (Call first)

Tennessee
53 Century Blvd., Suite 300
Nashville, TN 37214
Tel: 615-872-5855
Fax: 615-872-5899

Texas
815 Brazos Bldg., Suite 900
Austin, TX 78701
Tel: 512-476-9847
Fax: 512-478-6422

Utah
1756 East 10980 South
Sandy, UT 84092
Tel: 801-571-1171
Fax: 801-571-1271

Vermont
RR #1, Box 3517
Montpelier, VT 05602
Tel: 802-229-9478
Fax: 802-229-2745

Virginia
700 E. Main Street
Suite #1623
Richmond, VA 23219
Tel: 804-643-0043
Fax: 804-788-0447

Washington
509 East 12th Ave., Suite 8
Olympia, WA 98501
Tel: 206-786-8675
Fax: 206-943-2456

West Virginia
2253 Miller Road
Huntington, WV 25701
Tel: 304-529-3471
Fax: 304-529-3471 (Call first)

Wisconsin
119 M.L. King, Jr. Blvd.
Suite 516
Madison, WI 53703
Tel: 608-255-6083
Fax: 608-255-4909

Wyoming
1805 Capitol Ave., Suite 201
Cheyenne, WY 82001
Tel: 307-778-4045
Fax: 307-638-3469

NFIB Board of Directors

James S. Herr
Herr Foods, Inc.
Box 300
Nottingham, PA 19362

Susan A. Andrews
Brookside Properties, Inc.
224 White Bridge Road
Nashville, TN 37209

Ramon E. Billeaud
J.B. Levert Land Co.
P.O. Box 19245
New Orleans, LA 70179

Richard S. Briggs
307 Olive Hill Lane
Woodside, CA 94062

S. Jackson Faris
NFIB
53 Century Blvd., Suite 300
Nashville, TN 37214

Bruce G. Fielding, C.P.A.
Fielding & Associates
246A Center Avenue
Aptos, CA 95003

Mary F. Kelley
Strait, Kushinsky and
Company
1050 17th Street, Suite 1900
Denver, CO 80265-1901

Richard L. Reinhardt
PII Affiliates, Ltd.
P.O. Box 577
Manchester, PA 17345

Sidney T. Small
Sidmar Enterprises, Inc.
Two Kleen Way
Holbrook, MA 02343

William G. Thornton Jr.
Thornton Gardens
510 East U.S. 22 & 3
Maineville, OH 45039

Effective Letter Writing

O.K., so you've decided to get involved. To take personal measures to influence pro-small business public policy. But how do you make sure out of the thousands of letters a public official receives, your letter makes an impression? The following guidelines should help you:

• Timeliness Counts.

Very often, you can help a legislator form opinions on new legislation if you write a thoughtful, well-reasoned letter during the early stages of deliberation on a bill. It is more likely, however, that you will hear about pending legislation just before it is up for a vote. It is at this time that a quick response on your part will actually affect the outcome of the legislative roll call.

• Identify Yourself.

Use your business or personal letterhead whenever possible, providing your full name, business name, address and telephone number. Type your full name just below your signature. Use your judgment about which aspects of your background will most interest your legislator. For example, you might say, " I have owned my business for 25 years and have employed more than 150 local people during that time, so I understand the issues facing small business."

If you are a member of a trade association or other organization, such as the NFIB, that supports your views, mention it. For example, you might say, "I'm a member of the Printers Association of America and its position on workers' compensation is the same as mine."

• Style Matters.

When lobbying for your cause, take the time to address the public official by his or her proper title. The following is the correct way to address such officials:

President of the United States
The President
The White House
Washington, D.C.
Dear Mr. President:

Cabinet Secretary
The Honorable Jane Doe
Secretary of Commerce
U.S. Department of Commerce
Washington, D.C.
Dear Mr. Secretary:
Dear Madam Secretary:

U.S. Senator
The Honorable John Doe
United States Senate
Washington, D.C.
Dear Senator Doe:

U.S. Representative
The Honorable Jane Doe
U.S. House of Representatives
Washington, D.C.
Dear Congresswoman Doe:
Dear Congressman Doe:

Governor
The Honorable John Doe
Governor of Colorado
State House (or State Capitol)
Denver, Colorado
Dear Governor Doe:

State Legislator
The Honorable Jane Doe
Ohio House of Representatives
or Ohio State Senate
State House (or State Capitol)
Columbus, Ohio
Dear Senator Doe:
Dear Representative Doe:

Mayor
The Honorable John Doe
Mayor of Atlanta
City Hall
Atlanta, Georgia
Dear Mayor Doe:

Be sure to personalize your letter. You can even write it by hand, if it is legible; handwritten letters are often more effective than typed ones. State your case clearly and succinctly.

Don't try to address more than one issue per letter, and stick to the major points you wish to make about that issue.

Try to connect your topic with news items or some other timely issue. For example, you might say, "The national unemployment figures released yesterday indicate that we must do something to support small businesses, since they create two out of every three new jobs in this country."

• Know the Issue.

Write in your own words. An original letter always carries more weight than a form letter. If you are using arguments from NFIB or another lobbying organization's material, do not copy them verbatim. Change the wording, list the reasons in a different order, or choose one or two reasons and explain how they relate to your business and community.

It's also important to mention bill numbers if you are discussing legislation. (NFIB can help with details like these.) Quite often, several bills all relating to the same problem will be under consideration at the same time, and each bill will represent a slightly different approach to solving the problem.

• Know Whom to Contact.

It's best to write your own representative rather than someone from another area. Exceptions might occur when you write to someone who is running for the presidency or to someone who is on a committee studying the legislation or issue which concerns you.

• Positive Words.

Begin your letter with a commendation if at all appropriate, and maintain a calm, reasoned tone in your letter. People are naturally more receptive to constructive criticism than to harsh words. Therefore, a brief explanation of how you reached your conclusion and what alternatives are available are good points to include.

• Be Specific.

Tell your legislator exactly what action you would like taken on the issue, whether it involves voting a certain way or introducing specific legislation. A summary or conclusion will ensure that your remarks are clearly understood and not subject to misinterpretation.

• Following Through is Key.

A follow-up letter is crucial whenever you've had contact with your legislator. Legislators often have standard letters they send in response to contacts from their constituents. When you follow up their standard letters and highlight points they've made in them, you force them to think further and respond to you again.

For example, you may receive a letter from your legislator that states, "I agree with you that escalating health insurance premiums are a problem. But until we can control the inflation of medical costs, we will not see a decrease in premiums."

You could respond to that letter as follows: "Thank you, Congressman Doe, for your letter. I appreciated your thoughts about escalating health care costs; however, did you know that …"

When your legislator casts a vote that supports your position, always follow up with a letter of appreciation. A follow-up letter in this case will let the elected official know that you're aware of how he or she voted on the issues.

Be sure to keep copies of your letters and responses, and please forward copies of them to lobbying organizations you support, such as NFIB.

Opinions of Small Business Owners On Key Issues Being Decided in Government

N FIB is famous for standing by its committment to "ask before we act." That means the organization's position on issues affecting its members is not decided by a small group of board members, but by a vote of the entire membership. Being a member of NFIB means truly combining your voice with those of other small business owners just like you and having your message communicated directly to your state and national leaders. NFIB speaks for its members, it does not make their choices for them – something NFIB opposes in all levels of government.

Several times each year, NFIB sends surveys to each of its more than 600,000 members to obtain their opinions on a variety of public policy issues that directly affect them and their businesses. The response to these "Mandate" surveys is tremendous, discounting any claims from adversaries that small business owners are a "narrow special interest group."

The following are the results of several recent Mandate surveys showing how NFIB members regard some of the key issues facing the United States today.

The Budget, the Deficit & Taxes

Should small business owners receive a subsidy for hiring welfare recipients? (Mandate 504)

> Favor: 35%
> Oppose: 52%
> Undecided: 13%

Should employers be given a payroll tax credit for training new employees? (Mandate 503)

> Favor: 62%
> Oppose: 29%
> Undecided: 9%

Should banks be allowed to pool and sell small business loans to the securities market? (Mandate 502)

> Favor: 33%
> Oppose: 45%
> Undecided: 22%

Should congressional elections be publicly financed? (Mandate 502)

> Favor: 11%
> Oppose: 80%
> Undecided: 9%

Should the minimum wage be increased? (Mandate 502)

> Favor: 12%
> Oppose: 83%
> Undecided: 5%

Should the minimum wage be indexed for inflation? (Mandate 501)

> Favor: 16%
> Oppose: 78%
> Undecided: 6%

Should taxpayers be allowed to designate up to 10% of their tax payment to reduce the deficit? (Mandate 501)

> Favor: 78%
> Oppose: 14%
> Undecided: 8%

Should entitlement programs be subject to budget caps? (Mandate 500)

> Favor: 72%
> Oppose: 16%
> Undecided: 12%

Should small businesses be removed from superfund liability in exchange for a nominal fee? (Mandate 500)

> Favor: 31%
> Oppose: 48%
> Undecided: 21%

Should capital gains be taxed at death? (Mandate 500)

> Favor: 4%
> Oppose: 94%
> Undecided: 2%

Should Congress enact a new 1.5% payroll tax to be used for worker training programs? (Mandate 499)

> Favor: 2%
> Oppose: 95%
> Undecided: 3%

Should the salaries of members of Congress be linked to the federal budgetary process? (Mandate 498)

> Favor: 79%
> Oppose: 15%
> Undecided: 6%

Should retailers be allowed to bypass brokers within the purchasing process? (Mandate 498)

> Favor: 52%
> Oppose: 25%
> Undecided: 23%

Should the top income-tax rates be increased to help meet next year's budget deficit target ?
(Mandate 483)

> Favor: 16%
> Oppose: 81%
> Undecided: 3%

Should a freeze be imposed on the federal budget?
(Mandate 479)

> Favor: 72%
> Oppose: 18%
> Undecided: 10%

Should reductions in the Department of Defense budget
be used to cut taxes?
(Mandate 485)

> Favor: 66%
> Oppose: 39%
> Undecided: 5%

Should Congress focus its attention primarily on: deficit
reduction, foreign affairs, domestic programs, or none of
the above?
(Mandate 491)

> Deficit reduction: 88%
> Domestic programs: 10%
> Foreign affairs: 1%
> None of the above: 1%

How should Congress reduce the deficit?
(Mandate 471)

> Tax stock transactions and cut spending: 19%
> Cut spending: 71%
> Increase the gasoline tax and cut spending: 8%
> None of the above: 2%

Should the federal gasoline tax be increased 15 to 20 cents per gallon to reduce the deficit? (Mandate 479)

> Favor: 23%
> Oppose: 71%
> Undecided: 6%

Should the investment tax credit be reinstated for small firms? (Mandate 495)

> Favor: 81%
> Oppose: 11%
> Undecided: 8%

Child Labor

Should child labor laws be strengthened?
(Mandate 489)

> Favor: 20%
> Oppose: 68%
> Undecided: 12%

Should individuals below the age of 18 be required to obtain work permits? (Mandate 494)

> Favor: 22%
> Oppose: 70%
> Undecided: 8%

Employee Benefits

Should part-time workers be entitled to partial benefits?
(Mandate 501)

> Favor: 11%
> Oppose: 83%
> Undecided: 6%

Should the dollar limits on damage awards in employment discrimination cases be retained?
(Mandate 499)

> Favor: 92%
> Oppose: 5%
> Undecided: 3%

Should part-time employees get the same benefits as full-time employees? (Mandate 497)

> Favor: 7%
> Oppose: 90%
> Undecided: 3%

Should employers be required to provide unpaid parental and disability leave? (Mandate 479)

> Favor: 9%
> Oppose: 84%
> Undecided: 7%

Should a tax deduction be given to employers who offer parental leave as an employee benefit? (Mandate 479)

Favor: 35%
Oppose: 57%
Undecided: 8%

Should employers be required to provide unpaid family and medical leave to their employees?
(Mandate 499)

Favor: 13%
Oppose: 80%
Undecided: 7%

Should Congress establish a minimum uniform maternity leave standard? (Mandate 481)

Favor: 9%
Oppose: 83%
Undecided: 8%

Environment

Should the government be able to restrict the use of private land to protect the environment?
(Mandate 499)

Favor: 20%
Oppose: 69%
Undecided: 11%

Should polluters, including small businesses, be required to pay a fee to the Environmental Protection Agency that would be used to enforce the Clean Air Act?
(Mandate 484)

> Favor: 47%
> Oppose: 41%
> Undecided: 12%

Should small businesses cited for minor violations of the Clean Air Act have fines suspended for first offenses?
(Mandate 486)

> Favor: 78%
> Oppose: 17%
> Undecided: 5%

Should the Endangered Species Act be amended to include equal evaluation of economic and environmental impact? (Mandate 493)

> Favor: 55%
> Oppose: 31%
> Undecided: 14%

Should Congress enact a tax on materials that pollute the environment? (Mandate 497)

> Favor: 30%
> Oppose: 60%
> Undecided: 10%

Should businesses be required to label common products to indicate health and safety hazards? (Mandate 481)

> Favor: 39%
> Oppose: 50%
> Undecided: 11%

Should businesses be required to meet reduction goals for solid and hazardous waste? (Mandate 481)

> Favor: 48%
> Oppose: 36%
> Undecided: 16%

Should Congress require businesses to recycle a certain percentage of their solid waste? (Mandate 492)

> Favor: 34%
> Oppose: 57%
> Undecided: 9%

Health Care

Should health insurance purchasing groups be operated primarily by purchasers? (Mandate 503)

> Favor: 82%
> Oppose: 7%
> Undecided: 11%

Should independent contractors be treated as employees under the new health care system? (Mandate 504)

Favor: 5%
Oppose: 92%
Undecided: 3%

Should a VAT be used to pay for health care reform? (Mandate 502)

Favor: 9%
Oppose: 82%
Undecided: 9%

Should the medical portion of workers' compensation be moved into a new standard health plan? (Mandate 501)

Favor: 19%
Oppose: 63%
Undecided: 18%

Should individuals be permitted to fully deduct the cost of health care insurance if they are not covered by an employer plan? (Mandate 501)

Favor: 82%
Oppose: 11%
Undecided: 7%

Should individuals be required to obtain their own health insurance? (Mandate 500)

Favor: 51%
Oppose: 33%
Undecided: 16%

Should employers be required to provide health insurance for their employees? (Mandate 499)

Favor: 10%
Oppose: 85%
Undecided: 5%

Should Congress create a national board to oversee health care policy and spending? (Mandate 498)
Favor: 26%
Oppose: 60%
Undecided: 14%

Should employers be required to provide health insurance for their employees? (Mandate 470)

Favor: 8%
Oppose: 88%
Undecided: 4%

Should employers be required to provide health insurance for their employees? (Mandate 481)

Favor: 8%
Oppose: 88%
Undecided: 4%

Should employers with health insurance plans be required to cover former employees who have pre-existing conditions? (Mandate 479)

Favor: 10%
Oppose: 83%
Undecided: 7%

Should employers be required to offer health insurance without having to pay the premiums? (Mandate 494)

Favor: 30%
Oppose: 60%
Undecided: 10%

Should payroll taxes be increased to provide health coverage for the uninsured? (Mandate 483)

Favor: 4%
Oppose: 94%
Undecided: 2%

Should the federal government regulate the health insurance industry? (Mandate 491)

Favor: 23%
Oppose: 63%
Undecided: 14%

Should an individual income tax deduction for health insurance be restored? (Mandate 484)

Favor: 75%
Oppose: 17%
Undecided: 8%

If health insurance is mandated, should participants be taxed on the value of the premium? (Mandate 478)

Favor: 15%
Oppose: 81%
Undecided: 4%

Should the top corporate tax rate be increased to offset the cost of tax incentives for small business owners to offer health insurance? (Mandate 490)

> Favor: 20%
> Oppose: 70%
> Undecided: 10%

Labor

Should the Davis-Bacon Act be repealed? (Mandate 503)

> Favor: 81%
> Oppose: 9%
> Undecided: 10%

Should the government enter into "partnerships" with U.S. companies to develop new technologies?
(Mandate 504)

> Favor: 22%
> Oppose: 67%
> Undecided: 11%

Should the Davis-Bacon Act be extended to cover all sub-contractors and suppliers? (Mandate 496)

> Favor: 8%
> Oppose: 78%
> Undecided: 14%

Should Congress require employers to establish safety committees? (Mandate 496)

Favor: 6%
Oppose: 86%
Undecided: 8%

Should Congress enact a federal right-to-work law? (Mandate 497)

Favor: 62%
Oppose: 31%
Undecided: 7%

Occupational Health & Safety

Should employers be required to maintain written safety and health programs? (Mandate 504)

Favor: 7%
Oppose: 89%
Undecided: 4%

Should business owners be required to monitor and report the use of hazardous chemicals? (Mandate 498)

Favor: 30%
Oppose: 59%
Undecided: 11%

Should OSHA penalties be increased and minimum penalties be established to encourage compliance with safety and health regulations?
(Mandate 486)

Favor: 19%
Oppose: 72%
Undecided: 9%

Regulations Paperwork and Product Liability

Should EPA be required to undertake a comparison of risks and benefits when issuing new regulations?
(Mandate 504)

Favor: 68%
Oppose: 17%
Undecided: 15%

Should all existing federal regulations be reevaluated every three to five years? (Mandate 503)

Favor: 77%
Oppose: 11%
Undecided: 12%

Should the federal government be required to create a short form for all small business reporting requirements?
(Mandate 500)

Favor: 82%
Oppose: 9%
Undecided: 9%

Should the Paperwork Reduction Act apply to paperwork that the government requires business owners to retain? (Mandate 490)

Favor: 67%
Oppose: 13%
Undecided: 20%

Should federal agencies be required to assess whether a regulation could restrict the use of private property? (Mandate 490)

Favor: 64%
Oppose: 18%
Undecided: 18%

Should the Environmental Protection Agency be required to produce a "small business impact statement" when writing new environmental regulations? (Mandate 487)

Favor: 76%
Oppose: 13%
Undecided: 11%

Should Congress enact product liability reform? (Mandate 502)

Favor: 65%
Oppose: 20%
Undecided: 15%

Term Limits

Should insurance companies be allowed to enter into exclusive contracts? (Mandate 503)

> Favor: 15%
> Oppose: 74%
> Undecided: 11%

Should the number of congressional staff members be reduced? (Mandate 498)

> Favor: 94%
> Oppose: 3%
> Undecided: 3%

Should the Constitution be amended to limit the terms of U.S. Senators and Representatives? (Mandate 482)

> Favor: 66%
> Oppose: 26%
> Undecided: 8%

Congressional Directory

———

The following list of members of the 103rd Congress will help you decide to whom to send your correspondence.

The most effective way to contact your senator or representative is through his or her home office, where they are elected. We have listed the U.S. Capitol phone numbers of the 103rd Congress for a central reference. Central Washington addresses for senators and representatives are as follows:

U.S. Senate
Washington, D.C. 20510

U.S. House of Representatives
Washington, D.C. 20515

Alabama
Senate:

Howell Heflin (D)	202-224-4124
Richard C. Shelby (D)	202-224-5744

House:

1	Sonny Callahan (R)	202-225-4931
2	Terry Everett (R)	202-225-2901
3	Glen Browder (D)	202-225-3261
4	Tom Bevill (D)	202-225-4876
5	Bud Cramer (D)	202-225-4801

It is always better to contact your congressional representative in his or her home office. You will find that number in your local directory.

| 6 | Spencer Bachus (R) | 202-225-4921 |
| 7 | Earl Hilliard (D) | 202-225-2665 |

Alaska
Senate:
| Frank H. Murkowski (R) | 202-224-6665 |
| Ted Stevens (R) | 202-224-3004 |

House:
| At Large, Don Young (R) | 202-225-5765 |

Arizona
Senate:
| Dennis DeConcini (D) | 202-224-4521 |
| John McCain (R) | 202-224-2235 |

House:
1	Sam Coppersmith (D)	202-225-2635
2	Ed Pastor (D)	202-225-4065
3	Bob Stump (R)	202-225-4576
4	Jon Kyl (R)	202-225-3361
5	Jim Kolbe (R)	202-225-2542
6	Karan English (D)	202-225-2190

Arkansas
Senate:
| Dale L. Bumpers (D) | 202-224-4843 |
| David H. Pryor (D) | 202-224-2353 |

House:
1	Blanche Lambert (D)	202-225-3415
2	Ray Thornton (D)	202-225-2506
3	Tim Hutchinson (R)	202-225-4301
4	Jay Dickey (R)	202-225-3772

California
Senate:
| Barbara Boxer (D) | 202-224-3553 |
| Dianne Feinstein (D) | 202-224-3841 |

House:
1	Dan Hamburg (D)	202-225-3311
2	Wally Herger (R)	202-225-3076
3	Vic Fazio (D)	202-225-5716
4	John Doolittle (R)	202-225-2511
5	Robert T. Matsui (D)	202-225-7163

It is always better to contact your congressional representative in his or her home office. You will find that number in your local directory.

6	Lynn Woolsey (D)	202-225-5161
7	George Miller (D)	202-225-2095
8	Nancy Pelosi (D)	202-225-4965
9	Ronald V. Dellums (D)	202-225-2661
10	Bill Baker (R)	202-225-1880
11	Richard Pombo (R)	202-225-1947
12	Tom Lantos (D)	202-225-3531
13	Fortney Stark (D)	202-225-5065
14	Anna Eshoo (D)	202-225-8104
15	Norman Mineta (D)	202-225-2631
16	Don Edwards (D)	202-225-3072
17	Sam Farr (D)	202-225-2861
18	Gary Condit (D)	202-225-6131
19	Rick Lehman (D)	202-225-4540
20	Calvin Dooley (D)	202-225-3341
21	Bill Thomas (R)	202-225-2915
22	Michael Huffington (R)	202-225-3601
23	Elton Gallegly (R)	202-225-5811
24	Anthony C. Beilenson (D)	202-225-5911
25	Howard McKeon (R)	202-225-1956
26	Howard L. Berman (D)	202-225-4695
27	Carlos J. Moorhead (R)	202-225-4176
28	David Dreier (R)	202-225-2305
29	Henry A. Waxman (D)	202-225-3976
30	Xavier Becerra (D)	202-225-6235
31	Matthew G. Martinez (D)	202-225-5464
32	Julian C. Dixon (D)	202-225-7084
33	Lucille Roybal-Allard (D)	202-225-1766
34	Esteban Torres (D)	202-225-5256
35	Maxine Waters (D)	202-225-2201
36	Jane Harman (D)	202-225-8220
37	Walter Tucker (D)	202-225-7924
38	Steve Horn (R)	202-225-6676
39	Edward Royce (R)	202-225-4111
40	Jerry Lewis (R)	202-225-5861
41	Jay Kim (R)	202-225-3201
42	George Brown Jr. (D)	202-225-6161
43	Ken Calvert (R)	202-225-1986
44	Al McCandless (R)	202-225-5330
45	Dana Rohrabacher (R)	202-225-2415
46	Robert Dornan (R)	202-225-2965
47	Christopher Cox (R)	202-225-5611
48	Ron Packard (R)	202-225-3906
49	Lynn Schenk (D)	202-225-2040
50	Bob Filner (D)	202-225-8045
51	Randy Cunningham (R)	202-225-5452

It is always better to contact your congressional representative in his or her home office. You will find that number in your local directory.

| 52 | Duncan Hunter (R) | 202-225-5672 |

Colorado
Senate:

| Hank Brown (R) | 202-224-5941 |
| Ben Nighthorse Campbell (D) | 202-224-5852 |

House:

1	Pat Schroeder (D)	202-225-4431
2	David E. Skaggs (D)	202-225-2161
3	Scott McInnis (R)	202-225-4761
4	Wayne Allard (R)	202-225-4676
5	Joel M. Hefley (R)	202-225-4422
6	Dan Schaefer (R)	202-225-7882

Connecticut
Senate:

| Christopher J. Dodd (D) | 202-224-2823 |
| Joseph I. Lieberman (D) | 202-224-4041 |

House:

1	Barbara B. Kennelly (D)	202-225-2265
2	Sam Gejdenson (D)	202-225-2076
3	Rosa DeLauro (D)	202-225-3661
4	Christopher Shays (R)	202-225-5541
5	Gary Franks (R)	202-225-3822
6	Nancy Johnson (R)	202-225-4476

Delaware
Senate:

| Joseph R. Biden Jr. (D) | 202-224-5042 |
| William V. Roth Jr. (R) | 202-224-2441 |

House:

| At Large, Michael Castle (R) | 202-225-4165 |

Florida
Senate:

| Bob Graham (D) | 202-224-3041 |
| Connie Mack (R) | 202-224-5274 |

House:

1	Earl Hutto (D)	202-225-4136
2	Pete Peterson (D)	202-225-5235
3	Corrine Brown (D)	202-225-0123
4	Tillie Fowler (R)	202-225-2501

It is always better to contact your congressional representative in his or her home office. You will find that number in your local directory.

5	Karen Thurman (D)	202-225-1002
6	Clifford B. Stearns (R)	202-225-5744
7	John Mica (R)	202-225-4035
8	Bill McCollum (R)	202-225-2176
9	Michael Bilirakis (R)	202-225-5755
10	Bill Young (R)	202-225-5961
11	Sam M. Gibbons (D)	202-225-3376
12	Charles Canady (R)	202-225-1252
13	Dan Miller (R)	202-225-5015
14	Porter J. Goss (R)	202-225-2536
15	Jim Bacchus (D)	202-225-3671
16	Tom Lewis (R)	202-225-5729
17	Carrie Meek (D)	202-225-4506
18	Ileana Ros-Lehtinen (R)	202-225-3931
19	Harry A. Johnston II (D)	202-225-3001
20	Peter Deutsch (D)	202-225-7931
21	Lincoln Diaz-Balart (R)	202-225-4211
22	E. Clay Shaw Jr. (R)	202-225-3026
23	Alcee Hastings (D)	202-225-1313

Georgia
Senate:

Paul Coverdell (R)	202-224-3643
Sam Nunn (D)	202-224-3521

House:

1	Jack Kingston (R)	202-225-5831
2	Sanford Bishop (D)	202-225-3631
3	Mac Collins (R)	202-225-5901
4	John Linder (R)	202-225-4272
5	John Lewis (D)	202-225-3801
6	Newt Gingrich (R)	202-225-4501
7	Buddy Darden (D)	202-225-2931
8	J. Roy Rowland (D)	202-225-6531
9	Nathan Deal (D)	202-225-5211
10	Don Johnson (D)	202-225-4101
11	Cynthia McKinney (D)	202-225-1605

Hawaii
Senate:

Daniel K. Akaka (D)	202-224-6361
Daniel K. Inouye (D)	202-224-3934

House:

1	Neil Abercrombie (D)	202-225-2726
2	Patsy Mink (D)	202-225-4906

It is always better to contact your congressional representative in his or her home office. You will find that number in your local directory.

Idaho
Senate:

Larry E. Craig (R)	202-224-2752
Dirk Kempthorne (R)	202-224-6142

House:

1	Larry LaRocco (D)	202-225-6611
2	Michael Crappo (R)	202-225-5531

Illinois
Senate:

Carol Moseley Braun (D)	202-224-2854
Paul Simon (D)	202-224-2152

House:

1	Bobby Rush (D)	202-225-4372
2	Mel Reynolds (D)	202-225-0773
3	William Lipinski (D)	202-225-5701
4	Luis Gutierrez (D)	202-225-8203
5	Dan Rostenkowski (D)	202-225-4061
6	Henry J. Hyde (R)	202-225-4561
7	Cardiss Collins (D)	202-225-5006
8	Phillip M. Crane (R)	202-225-3711
9	Sidney R. Yates (D)	202-225-2111
10	John E. Porter (R)	202-225-4835
11	George Sangmeister (D)	202-225-3635
12	Jerry Costello (D)	202-225-5661
13	Harris Fawell (R)	202-225-3515
14	Dennis Hastert (R)	202-225-2976
15	Thomas Ewing (R)	202-225-2371
16	Donald Manzullo (R)	202-225-5676
17	Lane Evans (D)	202-225-5905
18	Robert H. Michel (R)	202-225-6201
19	Glenn Poshard (D)	202-225-5201
20	Richard J. Durbin (D)	202-225-5271

Indiana
Senate:

Dan Coats (R)	202-224-5623
Richard G. Lugar	202-224-4814

House:

1	Peter J. Visclosky (D)	202-225-2461
2	Phillip Sharp (D)	202-225-3021
3	Tim Roemer (D)	202-225-3915
4	Jill Long (D)	202-225-4436

It is always better to contact your congressional representative in his or her home office. You will find that number in your local directory.

5	Steve Buyer (R)	202-225-5037
6	Dan Burton (R)	202-225-2276
7	John T. Myers (R)	202-225-5805
8	Frank McCloskey (D)	202-225-4636
9	Lee H. Hamilton (D)	202-225-5315
10	Andrew Jacobs Jr. (D)	202-225-4011

Iowa
Senate:

| Charles E. Grassley (R) | 202-224-3744 |
| Tom Harkin (D) | 202-224-3254 |

House:

1	Jim Leach (R)	202-225-6576
2	Jim Nussle (R)	202-225-2911
3	Jim Lightfoot (R)	202-225-3806
4	Neal Smith (D)	202-225-4426
5	Fred Grandy (R)	202-225-5476

Kansas
Senate:

| Bob Dole (R) | 202-224-6521 |
| Nancy Landon Kassebaum (R) | 202-224-4774 |

House:

1	Pat Roberts (R)	202-225-2715
2	Jim Slattery (D)	202-225-6601
3	Jan Meyers (R)	202-225-2865
4	Dan Glickman (D)	202-225-6216

Kentucky
Senate:

| Wendell H. Ford (D) | 202-224-4343 |
| Mitch McConnell (R) | 202-224-2541 |

House:

1	Tom Barlow (D)	202-225-3115
2	William H. Natcher (D)	202-225-3501
3	Romano L. Mazzoli (D)	202-225-5401
4	Jim Bunning (R)	202-225-3465
5	Harold Rogers (R)	202-225-4601
6	Scotty Baesler (D)	202-225-4706

It is always better to contact your congressional representative in his or her home office. You will find that number in your local directory.

Louisiana
Senate:
John Breaux (D)	202-224-4623
J. Bennett Johnston (D)	202-224-5824

House:
1	Robert L. Livingston Jr. (R)	202-225-3015
2	William Jefferson (D)	202-225-6636
3	Billy Tauzin (D)	202-225-4031
4	Cleo Fields (D)	202-225-8490
5	Jim McCrery (R)	202-225-2777
6	Richard Baker (R)	202-225-3901
7	James A. Hayes (D)	202-225-2031

Maine
Senate:
William S. Cohen (R)	202-224-2523
George J. Mitchell (D)	202-224-5344

House
1	Thomas Andrews (D)	202-225-6116
2	Olympia J. Snowe (R)	202-225-6306

Maryland
Senate:
Barbara Mikulski (D)	202-224-4654
Paul Sarbanes (D)	202-224-4524

House:
1	Wayne Gilchrest (R)	202-225-5311
2	Helen Delich Bentley (R)	202-225-3061
3	Benjamin L. Cardin (D)	202-225-4016
4	Albert Wynn (D)	202-225-8699
5	Steny H. Hoyer (D)	202-225-4131
6	Roscoe Bartlett (R)	202-225-2721
7	Kweisi Mfume (D)	202-225-4741
8	Connie Morella (R)	202-225-5341

Massachusetts
Senate:
Edward M. Kennedy (D)	202-224-4543
John F. Kerry (D)	202-224-2742

House:
1	John Olver (D)	202-225-5335
2	Richard E. Neal (D)	202-225-5601

It is always better to contact your congressional representative in his or her home office. You will find that number in your local directory.

3	*Peter Blute (R)	202-225-6101
4	Barney Frank (D)	202-225-5931
5	*Martin Meehan (D)	202-225-3411
6	Peter Torkildsen (R)	202-225-8020
7	Edward J. Markey (D)	202-225-2836
8	Joseph P. Kennedy II (D)	202-225-5111
9	Joe Moakley (D)	202-225-8273
10	Gerry E. Studds (D)	202-225-3111

Michigan
Senate:

Carl Levin (D)	202-224-6221
Donald W. Riegle Jr. (D)	202-224-4822

House:

1	Bart Stupak (D)	202-225-4735
2	Peter Hoekstra (R)	202-225-4401
3	Vernon J. Ehlers (R)	202-225-3831
4	Dave Camp (R)	202-225-3561
5	James Barcia (D)	202-225-8171
6	Fred Upton (R)	202-225-3761
7	Nick Smith (R)	202-225-6276
8	Bob Carr (D)	202-225-4872
9	Dale Kildee (D)	202-225-3611
10	David Bonior (D)	202-225-2106
11	Joseph Knollenberg (R)	202-225-5802
12	Sander Levin (D)	202-225-4961
13	William Ford (D)	202-225-6261
14	John Conyers Jr. (D)	202-225-5126
15	Barbara-Rose Collins (D)	202-225-2261
16	John Dingell (D)	202-225-4071

Minnesota
Senate:

Dave Durenberger (R)	202-224-3244
Paul D. Wellstone (D)	202-224-5641

House:

1	Tim Penny (D)	202-225-2472
2	David Minge (D)	202-225-2331
3	Jim Ramstad (R)	202-225-2871
4	Bruce Vento (D)	202-225-6631
5	Martin Sabo (D)	202-225-4755
6	Rod Grams (R)	202-225-2271
7	Collin Peterson (D)	202-225-2165
8	James Oberstar (D)	202-225-6211

It is always better to contact your congressional representative in his or her home office. You will find that number in your local directory.

Mississippi
Senate:
Thad Cochran (R)   202-224-5054
Trent Lott (R)   202-224-6253

House
1   James Whitten (D)   202-225-4306
2   Bennie G. Thompson (D)   202-225-5876
3   Sonny Montgomery (D)   202-225-5031
4   Mike Parker (D)   202-225-5865
5   Gene Taylor (D)   202-225-5772

Missouri
Senate:
Christopher S. Bond (R)   202-224-5721
John C. Danforth (R)   202-224-6154

House:
1   William Clay Sr. (D)   202-225-2406
2   James Talent (R)   202-225-2561
3   Richard Gephardt (D)   202-225-2671
4   Ike Skelton (D)   202-225-2876
5   Alan Wheat (D)   202-225-4535
6   Pat Danner (D)   202-225-7041
7   Mel Hancock (R)   202-225-6536
8   Bill Emerson (R)   202-225-4404
9   Harold Volkmer (D)   202-225-2956

Montana
Senate:
Max Baucus (D)   202-224-2651
Conrad Burns (R)   202-224-2644

House:
At Large, Pat Williams (D)   202-225-3211

Nebraska
Senate:
James J. Exon (D)   202-224-4224
Robert J. Kerrey (D)   202-224-6551

House
1   Doug Bereuter (R)   202-225-4806
2   Peter Hoagland (D)   202-225-4155
3   Bill Barrett (R)   202-225-6435

It is always better to contact your congressional representative in his or her home office. You will find that number in your local directory.

194

Nevada
Senate:
Richard H. Bryan (D)	202-224-6244
Harry M. Reid (D)	202-224-3542

House
1	James H. Bilbray (D)	202-225-5965
2	Barbara F. Vucanovich (R)	202-225-6155

New Hampshire
Senate:
Judd Gregg (R)	202-224-3324
Bob Smith (R)	202-224-2841

House:
1	Bill Zeliff (R)	202-225-5456
2	Dick Swett (D)	202-225-5206

New Jersey
Senate:
Bill Bradley (D)	202-224-3224
Frank R. Lautenberg (D)	202-224-4744

House:
1	Robert Andrews (D)	202-225-6501
2	William J. Hughes (D)	202-225-6572
3	Jim Saxton (R)	202-225-4765
4	Christopher H. Smith (R)	202-225-3765
5	Marge Roukema (R)	202-225-4465
6	Frank Pallone Jr. (D)	202-225-4671
7	Bob Franks (R)	202-225-5361
8	Herbert Klein (D)	202-225-5751
9	Robert G. Torricelli (D)	202-225-5061
10	Donald M. Payne (D)	202-225-3436
11	Dean A. Gallo (R)	202-225-5034
12	Richard A. Zimmer (R)	202-225-5801
13	Robert Menendez (D)	202-225-7919

New Mexico
Senate:
Jeff Bingaman (D)	202-224-5521
Pete V. Domenici (R)	202-224-6621

House
1	Steven Schiff (R)	202-225-6316
2	Joe Skeen (R)	202-225-2365

It is always better to contact your congressional representative in his or her home office. You will find that number in your local directory.

3	Bill Richardson (D)	202-225-6190

New York
Senate:

Alfonse D'Amato (R)	202-224-6542
Daniel Patrick Moynihan (D)	202-224-4451

House:

1	George J. Hochbrueckner (D)	202-225-3826
2	Rick Lazio (R)	202-225-3335
3	Peter T. King (R)	202-225-7896
4	David Levy (R)	202-225-5516
5	Gary L. Ackerman (D)	202-225-2601
6	Floyd H. Flake (D)	202-225-3461
7	Thomas J. Manton (D)	202-225-3965
8	Jerrold Nadler (D)	202-225-5635
9	Charles E. Schumer (D)	202-225-6616
10	Edolphus Towns (D)	202-225-5936
11	Major R. Owens (D)	202-225-6231
12	Nydia Velazquez (D)	202-225-2361
13	Susan Molinari (R)	202-225-3371
14	Carolyn Maloney (D)	202-225-7944
15	Charles B. Rangel (D)	202-225-4365
16	Jose Serrano (D)	202-225-4361
17	Eliot L. Engel (D)	202-225-2464
18	Nita M. Lowey (D)	202-225-6506
19	Hamilton Fish Jr. (R)	202-225-5441
20	Benjamin A. Gilman (R)	202-225-3776
21	Michael R. McNulty (D)	202-225-5076
22	Gerald Solomon (R)	202-225-5614
23	Sherwood L. Boehlert (R)	202-225-3665
24	John McHugh (R)	202-225-4611
25	James T. Walsh (R)	202-225-3701
26	Maurice Hinchey (D)	202-225-6335
27	Bill Paxon (R)	202-225-5265
28	Louise M. Slaughter (D)	202-225-3615
29	John J. LaFalce (D)	202-225-3231
30	Jack Quinn (R)	202-225-3306
31	Amo Houghton Jr. (R)	202-225-3161

North Carolina
Senate:

Lauch Faircloth (R)	202-224-3154
Jesse Helms (R)	202-224-6342

It is always better to contact your congressional representative in his or her home office. You will find that number in your local directory.

House:
1   Eva Clayton (D)   202-225-3101
2   Tim Valentine (D)   202-225-4531
3   Martin Lancaster (D)   202-225-3415
4   David E. Price (D)   202-225-1784
5   Steve Neal (D)   202-225-2071
6   Howard Coble (R)   202-225-3065
7   Charles Rose III (D)   202-225-2731
8   Bill Hefner (D)   202-225-3175
9   Alex McMillan (R)   202-225-1976
10 Cass Ballenger (R)   202-225-2576
11 Charles Taylor (R)   202-225-6401
12 Melvin Watt (D)   202-225-1510

North Dakota
Senate:
Byron Dorgan (D)   202-224-2551
Kent Conrad (D)   202-224-2043

House:
At Large, Earl Pomeroy (D)   202-225-2611

Ohio
Senate:
John Glenn (D)   202-224-3353
Howard M. Metzenbaum (D)   202-224-2315

House:
1   David Mann (D)   202-225-2216
2   Rob Portman (R)   202-225-3164
3   Tony Hall (D)   202-225-6465
4   Michael G. Oxley (R)   202-225-2676
5   Paul Gillmor (R)   202-225-6405
6   Ted Strickland (D)   202-225-5705
7   David Hobson (R)   202-225-4324
8   John Boehner (R)   202-225-6205
9   Marcy Kaptur (D)   202-225-4146
10 Martin Hoke (R)   202-225-5871
11 Louis Stokes (D)   202-225-7032
12 John Kasich (R)   202-225-5355
13 Sherrod Brown (D)   202-225-3401
14 Thomas Sawyer (D)   202-225-5231
15 Deborah Pryce (R)   202-225-2015
16 Ralph Regula (R)   202-225-3876
17 James A. Traficant Jr. (D)   202-225-5261
18 Douglas Applegate (D)   202-225-6265

It is always better to contact your congressional representative in his or her home office. You will find that number in your local directory.

19	Eric Fingerhut (D)	202-225-5731

Oklahoma
Senate:

David L. Boren (D)	202-224-4721
Don Nickles (R)	202-224-5754

House:

1	James M. Inhofe (R)	202-225-2211
2	Mike Synar (D)	202-225-2701
3	Bill Brewster (D)	202-225-4565
4	Dave McCurdy (D)	202-225-6165
5	Earnest J. Istook, Jr. (R)	202-225-2132

Oregon
Senate:

Mark O. Hatfield (R)	202-224-3753
Bob Packwood (R)	202-224-5244

House:

1	Elizabeth Furse (D)	202-225-0855
2	Bob Smith (R)	202-225-6730
3	Ron Wyden (D)	202-225-4811
4	Peter DeFazio (D)	202-225-6416
5	Mike Kopetski (D)	202-225-5711

Pennsylvania
Senate:

Arlen Specter (R)	202-224-4254
Harris Wofford (D)	202-224-6324

House:

1	Thomas Foglietta (D)	202-225-4731
2	Lucien Blackwell (D)	202-225-4001
3	Robert Borski (D)	202-225-8251
4	Ron Klink (D)	202-225-2565
5	Bill Clinger Jr. (R)	202-225-5121
6	Tim Holden (D)	202-225-5546
7	Curt Weldon (R)	202-225-2011
8	Jim Greenwood (R)	202-225-4276
9	Bud Shuster (R)	202-225-2431
10	Joseph McDade (R)	202-225-3731
11	Paul E. Kanjorski (D)	202-225-6511
12	John Murtha (D)	202-225-2065
13	Marjorie Mezvinsky (D)	202-225-6111
14	William Coyne (D)	202-225-2301

It is always better to contact your congressional representative in his or her home office. You will find that number in your local directory.

15	Paul McHale (D)	202-225-6411
16	Robert S. Walker (R)	202-225-2411
17	George Gekas (R)	202-225-4315
18	Rick Santorum (R)	202-225-2135
19	William Goodling (R)	202-225-5836
20	Austin Murphy (D)	202-225-4665
21	Thomas Ridge (R)	202-225-5406

Rhode Island
Senate:

John H. Chafee (R)	202-224-2921
Claiborne Pell (D)	202-224-4642

House:

1	Ronald K. Machtley (R)	202-225-4911
2	Jack Reed (D)	202-225-2735

South Carolina
Senate:

Ernest F. Hollings (D)	202-224-6121
Strom Thurmond (R)	202-224-5972

House

1	Arthur Ravenel Jr. (R)	202-225-3176
2	Floyd Spence (R)	202-225-2452
3	Butler Derrick Jr. (D)	202-225-5301
4	Bob Inglis (R)	202-225-6030
5	John M. Spratt Jr. (D)	202-225-5501
6	James Clyburn (D)	202-225-3315

South Dakota
Senate:

Tom Daschle (D)	202-224-2321
Larry Pressler (R)	202-224-5842

House

At Large, Tim Johnson (D)	202-225-2801

Tennessee
Senate:

Jim Sasser (D)	202-224-3344
Harlan Mathews (D)	202-224-4944

House:

1	Jimmy Quillen (R)	202-225-6356
2	John J. Duncan Jr. (R)	202-225-5435

It is always better to contact your congressional representative in his or her home office. You will find that number in your local directory.

3	Marilyn Lloyd (D)	202-225-3271
4	Jim Cooper (D)	202-225-6831
5	Bob Clement (D)	202-225-4311
6	Bart Gordon (D)	202-225-4231
7	Don Sundquist (R)	202-225-2811
8	John S. Tanner (D)	202-225-4714
9	Harold E. Ford (D)	202-225-3265

Texas
Senate:

| Kay Bailey Hutchison (R) | 202-224-5922 |
| Phil Gramm (R) | 202-224-2934 |

House:

1	Jim Chapman (D)	202-225-3035
2	Charles Wilson (D)	202-225-2401
3	Sam Johnson (R)	202-225-4201
4	Ralph Hall (D)	202-225-6673
5	John Bryant (D)	202-225-2231
6	Joe Barton (R)	202-225-2002
7	Bill Archer (R)	202-225-2571
8	Jack Fields Jr. (R)	202-225-4901
9	Jack Brooks (D)	202-225-6565
10	Jake Pickle (D)	202-225-4865
11	Chet Edwards (D)	202-225-6105
12	Pete Geren (D)	202-225-5071
13	Bill Sarpalius (D)	202-225-3706
14	Greg Laughlin (D)	202-225-2831
15	E. (Kika) de la Garza (D)	202-225-2531
16	Ron Coleman (D)	202-225-4831
17	Charles Stenholm (D)	202-225-6605
18	Craig Washington (D)	202-225-3816
19	Larry Combest (R)	202-225-4005
20	Henry B. Gonzales (D)	202-225-3236
21	Lamar Smith (R)	202-225-4236
22	Tom DeLay (R)	202-225-5951
23	Henry Bonilla (R)	202-225-4511
24	Martin Frost (D)	202-225-3605
25	Mike A. Andrews (D)	202-225-7508
26	Dick Armey (R)	202-225-7772
27	Solomon Ortiz (D)	202-225-7742
28	Frank Tejeda (D)	202-225-1640
29	Gene Green (D)	202-225-1688
30	Eddie Bernice Johnson (D)	202-225-8885

It is always better to contact your congressional representative in his or her home office. You will find that number in your local directory.

Utah
Senate:
Robert Bennett (R)   202-224-5444
Orrin G. Hatch (R)   202-224-5251

House:
1   James V. Hansen (R)   202-225-0453
2   Karen Shepherd (D)   202-225-3011
3   William Orton (D)   202-225-7751

Vermont
Senate:
James Jeffords (R)   202-224-5141
Patrick Leahy (D)   202-224-4242

House:
At Large, Bernie Sanders (O)   202-225-4115

Virginia
Senate:
Charles S. Robb (D)   202-224-4024
John Warner (R)   202-224-2023

House:
1   Herbert H. Bateman (R)   202-225-4261
2   Owen B. Pickett (D)   202-225-4215
3   Robert Scott (D)   202-225-8351
4   Norman Sisisky (D)   202-225-6365
5   Lewis F. Payne Jr. (D)   202-225-4711
6   Robert Goodlatte (R)   202-225-5431
7   Thomas J. Bliley Jr. (R)   202-225-2815
8   James Moran (D)   202-225-4376
9   Rick Boucher (D)   202-225-3861
10 Frank R. Wolf (R)   202-225-5136
11 Leslie Byrne (D)   202-225-1492

Washington
Senate:
Slade Gorton (R)   202-224-3441
Patty Murray (D)   202-224-2621

House:
1   Maria Cantwell (D)   202-225-6311
2   Al Swift (D)   202-225-2605
3   Jolene Unsoeld (D)   202-225-3536
4   Jay Inslee (D)   202-225-5816

It is always better to contact your congressional representative in his or her home office. You will find that number in your local directory.

5	Thomas S. Foley (D)	202-225-2006
6	Norman D. Dicks (D)	202-225-5916
7	Jim McDermott (D)	202-225-3106
8	Jennifer Dunn (R)	202-225-7761
9	Mike Kreidler (D)	202-225-8901

West Virginia
Senate:
Robert C. Byrd (D)   202-224-3954
John D. Rockefeller IV (D)   202-224-6472

House:
1	Alan B. Mollohan (D)	202-225-4172
2	Bob Wise Jr. (D)	202-225-2711
3	Nick Joe Rahall II (D)	202-225-3452

Wisconsin
Senate:
Russell Feingold (D)   202-224-5323
Herb Kohl (D)   202-224-5653

House:
1	Peter W. Barca (D)	202-225-3031
2	Scott Klug (R)	202-225-2906
3	Steve Gunderson (R)	202-225-5506
4	Gerald D. Kleczka (D)	202-225-4572
5	Thomas Barrett (D)	202-225-3571
6	Thomas E. Petri (R)	202-225-2476
7	David R. Obey (D)	202-225-3365
8	Toby Roth (R)	202-225-5665
9	Jim Sensenbrenner (R)	202-225-5101

Wyoming
Senate:
Alan K. Simpson (R)   202-224-3424
Malcolm Wallop (R)   202-224-6441

House
At Large, Craig Thomas (R)   202-225-2311

It is always better to contact your congressional representative in his or her home office. You will find that number in your local directory.

NFIB Membership Enrollment Form

Join the fight for small business!
Join NFIB today.

 Suite 300
53 Century Blvd.
Nashville, TN 37214

For information about joining NFIB, photocopy this page, complete
the form below and mail it to the above address.
Or you may call 1-800-NFIB-NOW

Name_____
        First Name   Middle Initial   Last Name

Firm Name_____

Business Address_____

City_____State_____ZIP_____

Business Phone (   )_____ No. of Employees_____

Type of Business_____